ISBN 978-1-332-35114-5
PIBN 10317501

# 1 MONTH OF
# FREE
# READING

## at

## www.ForgottenBooks.com

By purchasing this book you are eligible for one month membership to ForgottenBooks.com, giving you unlimited access to our entire collection of over 700,000 titles via our web site and mobile apps.

To claim your free month visit:

www.forgottenbooks.com/free317501

English
Français
Deutsche
Italiano
Español
Português

# www.forgottenbooks.com

**Mythology** Photography **Fiction**
Fishing Christianity **Art** Cooking
Essays Buddhism Freemasonry
Medicine **Biology** Music **Ancient
Egypt** Evolution Carpentry Physics
Dance Geology **Mathematics** Fitness
Shakespeare **Folklore** Yoga Marketing
**Confidence** Immortality Biographies
Poetry **Psychology** Witchcraft
Electronics Chemistry History **Law**
Accounting **Philosophy** Anthropology
Alchemy Drama Quantum Mechanics
Atheism Sexual Health **Ancient History**
**Entrepreneurship** Languages Sport
Paleontology Needlework Islam
**Metaphysics** Investment Archaeology
Parenting Statistics Criminology
**Motivational**

# BEASTS AND MEN

BEING CARL HAGENBECK'S EXPERIENCES
FOR HALF A CENTURY AMONG
WILD ANIMALS

AN ABRIDGED TRANSLATION

BY

HUGH S. R. ELLIOT

AND

A. G. THACKER, A.R.C.S. (LOND.)

WITH AN INTRODUCTION BY

P. CHALMERS MITCHELL, M.A., D.Sc., LL.D., F.R.S.

SECRETARY OF THE ZOOLOGICAL SOCIETY OF LONDON

WITH PHOTOGRAVURE PORTRAIT OF THE AUTHOR
AND NINETY-NINE OTHER ILLUSTRATIONS

SECOND IMPRESSION

LONGMANS, GREEN, AND CO.

39 PATERNOSTER ROW, LONDON
NEW YORK, BOMBAY, AND CALCUTTA
1910

Fs

# INTRODUCTION.

Soon after I became Secretary of the Zoological Society of London, there called on me a tall, lean man, with a bony weather-beaten face, shaven lips and a short, grizzled beard of the kind known as a "chin-fringe". His shrewd and kindly face, slow speech with nasal intonations and general air of confident but watchful friendliness made the impression of an individuality very unlike the composite photograph I have in my mind of the Germans I know. But for the presence of a German accent and the absence of the tobacco habit, Carl Hagenbeck might pass for a New England ship captain. He is in the first place a business man with a strong spirit of adventure that must have led him into many losses, and as he has none the less built up a great and successful business, it must be supposed that he also knows how to make profits. But those who deal with him soon learn that they may rely implicitly on his directness and candour in arranging a purchase or sale, and on his scrupulous carefulness in carrying out his share of the bargain. On one occasion, for instance, I had to arrange with him for the purchase of a pair of hippopotamus which neither of us had seen. The price was to depend partly on the age of the animals, but as that could not be proved, we agreed on a standard of size. When the animals arrived, although in every other respect equally suitable, they were a little smaller than Hagenbeck had been led to expect by his agents, but without demur he at once agreed to the corresponding reduction in price. Mr. Hagenbeck, however, takes much more than a business interest in his business, and I am glad to have the opportunity of acknowledging with all gratitude his readiness to place the results of his long experience at the service of the Zoological Society of London. Again and again he has given me information of great value on questions relating to the transport and housing of animals and on their feeding and treatment. It is a pleasure to me to introduce to English readers a book in which is displayed so many of the strange experiences and so much of the remarkable personality of this most interesting man.

Every one has seen something of the business of a dealer in animals in its primitive form. Near the London Docks, and on the quays of great shipping ports like Havre and Marseilles, there are to be found untidy and generally evil smelling little shops crowded with parrots and monkeys, and similar casual acquisitions from sailors. The proprietors tend to become importers in a small way. They find out what creatures they can sell most readily, and give orders to sailors or petty officers, sometimes on speculation and sometimes at the request of customers. With a few notable exceptions, however, such small dealers never learn their trade. The birds and mammals they obtain have in many cases been improperly fed and very badly packed, with the result that the mortality is great and the stamina of the survivors is at a low ebb. There can be no doubt but that in many cases the reputation for delicacy acquired by many exotic birds and mammals is due merely to the senseless fashion in which they are brought home. They are captured in some tropical forest and rushed down to the coast with a minimum supply of what is supposed to be their natural food. The transition to strange food is made under the worst conditions, on board ship or in the dealer's shop, or in the unfamiliar surroundings of a new home.  A golden rule in the purchase of animals with which one is not fully acquainted, is to refuse them unless they feed readily on a kind of food which the purchaser can supply in future.  Such a condition may be fulfilled most easily when the animals, immediately after they are caught, are accustomed gradually to a new diet and to take their food from human beings.  In the vast majority of cases it is change of food and not change of climate that is the difficulty in what is called acclimatisation.  Walruses are brought to a European city with an appetite for nothing but whales' blubber, or monkeys who refuse everything except fresh sugar-cane, and the usual tragedies result.

Carl Hagenbeck's business is conducted on very different lines, and the animals he imports and distributes have been treated so as to have the best chance of surviving. He has been a notable pioneer in the proper handling of wild animals.  He is an able man, and sees that the crude methods do not pay ; he is a naturalist with a genuine affection and sympathy for animals, and in all his handling of them he sees to it that their health and general condition is the first care.  In the many expeditions he has organised to Africa and Asia for the capture of wild animals, the highest qualities of a naturalist have been necessary.  It is the fashion to claim that the big game sportsman and collector of trophies must be a naturalist of a high order ; I have heard defenders of these forms of sport speak as if the poet Coleridge had written :—

> He killeth best who loveth best,
> All things both great and small.

There was perhaps the beginning of a defence for such a

point of view before rifles were so perfect and deadly as they are now and when the hunter had to wage his own life against that of his quarry, and could have small hope of success without the most intimate knowledge of the habits of wild animals. The modern hunters who must be genuine naturalists are those who attempt to photograph big game in their native resorts and those who wish to catch them alive and uninjured.

English readers interested in Zoological Gardens will turn with avidity to the account Carl Hagenbeck gives of the Zoological Park at Stellingen. The fundamental conception which for long dominated the minds of those who had to do with the exhibition of living animals was a compromise between the idea of a travelling menagerie and the idea of a museum. The specimens were ranged in narrow and small cages so that they might be easily seen and compared. Iron bars and wire-work were everywhere in evidence, and so far as possible all draught and fresh air were excluded, and elaborate heating-systems were provided. In Hagenbeck's Park, which is the result of his long experience, these old ideas are discarded. The animals are given shelters to which they can retreat, and in these some amount of artificial heat is supplied in severe weather, but in every case room for exercise, abundant fresh air, and free exposure to rain and sun are provided for. I do not think that there is any doubt as to these being the right lines, and all the more progressive Zoological Gardens have been trying to act on them. No doubt the ideal condition is the right temperature as well as relative freedom and exposure to fresh air, but if the choice has to be made, and it must be made in the cities of Europe and North America, then fresh air is enormously more important than temperature, and animals that we are accustomed to think of as tropical thrive well and freely disport themselves in snow and rain. I am not so certain that I agree with some of the other characteristic features of the Park at Stellingen, but they are at the least extremely interesting. The grouping of incongruous animals in "happy families" is perhaps more the work of the showman than of the naturalist. It is always subject to very serious risks, and success can be obtained only in the case of young animals specially trained to disregard their natural instincts. It is a curious and interesting spectacle, but not one that I should like to see repeated in ordinary menageries and Zoological Gardens.

On the other hand, the devices by which bars and railings are replaced by ditches and undercut ledges of rockwork are extremely attractive, and to my mind pleasing, although I do not much care for the more exuberant forms of such artificial scenery with painted backgrounds. Where the necessary space can be obtained, it is delightful to see animals across ditches instead of through bars. But there is another side to the question. If visitors are to be protected, the arrangements must be such that the animals are seen from a considerably greater distance, and it is doubtful, especially in the case of the larger Carnivora, if the arrangement is practicable except with trained animals. Diversifying the ground with artificial rockwork on which the animals may climb certainly adds very much to the beauty of the display, and the additional exercise given to the animals must be a great advantage. But here again there is another side to the question. Rockwork, natural or artificial, is extremely difficult to keep in the state of sanitary cleanliness which is essential in a menagerie, and it provides a cover most attractive to rats and from which it is almost impossible to dislodge them. The abundant supplies of food always attract rats to Zoological Gardens, of which they are the most troublesome pest, and the only way of keeping them down is to afford them the least opportunity of finding cover. The various difficulties and objections that I suggest, however, although they may prevent other gardens from following the example set by Carl Hagenbeck, do not detract from the extreme interest of his description of Stellingen.

For many years Hagenbeck has been the greatest trainer of animals, and his own troupes or those which he has supplied have appeared in every part of the world. Lovers of animals will follow with a close attention his method of selecting and training them. For my own part, and I know of many who share my views, I seldom lose an opportunity of seeing exhibitions of performing animals, and equally seldom do I enjoy the performance for long except perhaps in the case of sea-lions, who appear to me to enjoy what they are doing. In all other cases I gradually become convinced that abject terror of the trainer lies behind the tricks, a conviction that is not disturbed by the rewards of food that are given. This, however, is not Mr. Hagenbeck's opinion, and his love of animals, ability and experience entitle him to the fullest consideration. He begins with the proposition, long ago set out by Darwin, that the first business of the trainer is to select his animals. Individuals have very different dispositions, and it is only one or two out of many that have the power of attention, ability and docility required by the trainer. Thereafter the method is little more than constant patience, firmness and kindness on the part of the trainer. I accept readily Mr. Hagenbeck's statements as to his personal control over wild animals, and I have myself seen many instances of their friendly recognition of their old master. But with regard to public performances, when the animals have to go through their tricks at stated

times, I continue to doubt ; in all those that I have seen the
trainer displays some kind of whip, and the animals seem to
have a very full appreciation that it is more than a symbol of
authority.

Although I can take no credit, and have no responsibility
for the form in which this edition is presented to English
readers, I have had some opportunity of comparing it with the
German text, and believe it to be a very accurate rendering
of the substance of a remarkable book.

P. CHALMERS MITCHELL.

# CONTENTS

# CHAPTER I.

## MY LIFE IN THE ANIMAL TRADE.

THE great zoological park at Stellingen, and the huge trade in living animals of which that park is the headquarters, had a very humble and almost accidental origin. My father was a fishmonger trading in St. Pauli, a suburb of Hamburg, and one day in March, 1848, it happened that some of the fishermen, whom my father employed, and who were under contract to deliver over to him their entire haul, captured in their nets no fewer than six seals. My father was very fond of animals and greatly interested in natural history, and thus it occurred to him that the curiosity with which he himself examined the animals might, perhaps, be shared by his fellow-citizens of Hamburg, and that the interest which the seals would probably arouse could be made profitable to their owner. He therefore exhibited the creatures in two huge wooden tubs at our house in Spielbudenplatz, St. Pauli, charging an entrance fee of one Hamburg shilling (= about a penny) per head. A considerable number of people came to inspect the beasts, and my father was so delighted at the success of his idea that he decided to follow up this new line of business and take the seals to Berlin. To those who know the twentieth-century Berlin the idea of taking a few common seals to be exhibited in that city will no doubt appear extremely ludicrous; but the Berliners of those days were very much less sophisticated than their modern representatives, and flocked with great interest to see my father's show. Owing to the revolutionary movement which was at that time daily growing in force, my father did not remain for long in the Prussian capital, but sold his seals and returned home to Hamburg. Unfortunately the animals were not sold for hard cash, but were handed over on the strength of a promise of future payment—a promise which completely slipped the memory of the purchaser—but in spite of this there was, owing to the great success of the exhibitions both in Hamburg and in Berlin, a considerable profit on the whole transaction, and my father was far from dissatisfied with his new venture.

From the time of this seal incident onwards my father commenced to carry on a trade in living animals, in addition to his work as a purveyor of food-fish. Indeed, although he had never before thought of making any money out of it, he already possessed a small menagerie, including goats, a cow, a monkey, a talking parrot, fowls, geese, etc., to which some more common seals, a polar bear, hyænas, and other mammals and birds were presently added. The little menagerie was set up in Spielbudenplatz, and visitors were charged an entrance fee of four Hamburg shillings. My father did not again travel about exhibiting his seals, but sold them to the owners of itinerant circuses and menageries, by whom they used to be shown to a credulous and unscientific public as walruses, or even as mermaids!

Thus from my earliest childhood I was accustomed to dealing with living animals. I was born on the 10th of June, 1844, and had two brothers and three sisters. My mother died in 1865, and, my father marrying a second time, I subsequently had two half-brothers, John Hagenbeck of Colombo, Ceylon, and Gustav Hagenbeck, who still resides in Hamburg. My early education was somewhat meagre, for I only went to school when I could spare the time from my work with the fish and live beasts, and this did not amount to more than three months in the year. It was not that my father failed to appreciate the benefits of a good education; on the contrary, he deemed a great part of the customary instruction thoroughly necessary. But he was an eminently practical

Seals having a bath.

man, and whilst he impressed upon us the urgency of learn_
ing well the "Three R's," he used to tell us that we "were
not expected to become parsons". Later on, too, when our
business began to extend to France and England, he saw
that it would be desirable for me to acquire the languages of
those countries. Thus, although my elementary education
may have left something to be desired, from my twelfth
year onwards I attended school with greater regularity, and
in my later boyhood gained a considerable knowledge of lan_
guages and other more advanced subjects.

As the business gradually developed, it became necessary
to undertake journeys for the purpose of buying and selling
our living wares, and I soon discovered that the transport
of wild beasts is apt to be rich in incident. I well remember
my first expedition of the kind. One day when I was eleven
years old we heard that there was a small collection of animals
to be sold at Bremerhaven. At that time a journey to Bremerhaven was quite an undertaking, for there was then no
direct railway connection between that town and Hamburg,
and it was therefore necessary either to go a long journey
round by Hanover, or else to drive across country to Bremen, a distance of about fifty miles. Notwithstanding this
difficulty, however, my father, being anxious to acquire the
animals, decided to go to Bremerhaven, and he took me with
him. We found that the little menagerie consisted of a large
racoon, two American opossums, and a varied assortment of
monkeys and parrots. My father purchased the lot, and
after they had been brought up to Bremen by steamer
they were duly ensconced upon the roof of the diligence
which was to convey us back to Hamburg.

We drove all through the night, our route lying across the
Lüneburger Heath, a wild stretch of country in the north of
Hanover, and daybreak found us in Harburg, a place not
far from Hamburg. Naturally, our first thought was to
inspect our property and see that all was safe. Great was
our dismay when we found the racoon's cage broken open

and its erstwhile occupant completely vanished! During the
night the racoon must have made his way out through the
bars, and have jumped off the top of the coach.

We dared not give the alarm, for, unless the fugitive had
been speedily recaptured, we should have had the authorities
down on us for letting loose wild beasts in the heart of
Germany. So we all kept our own counsel, and nobody
knew of the occurrence save my father, the driver of the
diligence, and myself. Two years later, however, it was
noised abroad that a racoon had been killed on Lüneburger
Heath, and there was great excitement in the newspapers
and much speculation as to how that carnivore came to be
living wild in Germany. We might have been able to
suggest a not improbable solution of the mystery, but we
judged it more discreet to hold our tongues.

In our early days we had many similar mishaps, most of
them taking place at home, however. On one occasion we
were aroused in the middle of the night by a terrified night-
watchman, who informed us that an enormous seal was
perambulating the streets of Hamburg. We rushed out
with nets, and just succeeded in securing the creature as it
was about to return to its native element. On another
occasion a hyæna escaped from its cage, and was only
recaptured after a long, and decidedly dangerous, nocturnal
hunt.

Such episodes as these, however, only formed occasional
diversions. My chief recollection of the first ten years of the
business is that it was a ceaseless round of very hard, and
not over-profitable, work. We had to buy our experience
dearly, and almost every mistake that we made in the treatment of the beasts, or in the methods of transporting them,
would cost us the lives of some of the creatures. Indeed, for
part of the time, my father ran the business at a loss, and
if his success as a fishmonger had not enabled him to pass
through this black period, it is highly probable that he would
have given up the animal trade altogether. This, however,

together with his fondness of the animals for their own sake, induced him to persevere; and as by our repeated failures we gradually came to understand better the requirements of our pets, the death rate in the menagerie steadily diminished, and the profits on the business rose accordingly.

It was not until nine years after the foundation of the business, in 1857 that is, that my father purchased his first large collection of animals. This consisted of five lions, a number of panthers and cheetahs, several hyænas and various antelopes, gazelles and monkeys, all of which the African explorer, Dr. Natterer, had brought back to Vienna from the Egyptian Sudan, a region which was at that time extraordinarily rich in animal life. In the following year my father one day asked me seriously, whether I would choose as my future calling to be a fishmonger or an animal dealer, and, after placing all the pros and cons before me, he finally advised me to take up fishmongering as being the less speculative trade. I am sure, however, that he did this with a heavy heart, for we all loved our menagerie; and when I decided in favour of the animal business he showed no displeasure, but immediately gave his consent to this course of action. It was arranged, therefore, that I should take over responsibility for the business, and that my father's liability in the event of any future loss should not exceed £100. I left school in March, 1859—before I turned fifteen—and from that day to this I have devoted all my energies to the care and development of the business which my father founded. The latter, however, remained until his death my most trusted adviser, and if in my life's work I have attained to some measure of success, it is to him that much of the credit is due. From our earliest years he taught us to love animals and helped us to understand their needs and their instincts. This has assuredly been the cornerstone of all our success, for without a genuine love for animals a business such as ours must have inevitably failed.

During the latter half of the nineteenth century Africa
was being vigorously explored, and large consignments of
animals—especially elephants, giraffes and rhinoceroses—
began to arrive in Europe from that continent.   In the
early sixties we began to deal on a larger scale, and I
frequently had to undertake journeys for business purposes,
my first visit to England being in 1864.   The trade became
more flourishing, necessitating an extension of our premises
in Spielbudenplatz, and in this same year of 1864 an important
development occurred.   Late one evening we received a
telegram from a friend in Vienna, saying that the African
traveller, Lorenzo Cassanova, had arrived in the Austrian
capital *en route* for Dresden, whither he was taking a number
of animals which he had collected in Nubia.   About a year
and a half earlier Cassanova had brought home an enormous
consignment of wild beasts from the Egyptian Sudan, including the first African elephant which had ever been seen in
Europe, several giraffes, and numerous smaller creatures.

Gottlieb Kreutzberg.

On that occasion we could not afford
to buy his collection, and the animals
were eventually acquired by the
famous old menagerie owner, Gottlieb
Kreutzberg ; but this time the collection was much smaller, and on the
morning after the receipt of the telegram I set out for Dresden.   I found
Cassanova in the Zoological Gardens,
where he had housed his animals, and
before long the whole collection had
come into my possession.   This, how-
ever, was not the only or the most important result of my
meeting with the Italian ; for after some discussion we concluded an agreement to the effect that all the animals which
Cassanova succeeded in bringing to Europe from his future
expeditions should be sold to us at definite prices named in
the contract.   Cassanova was thus the first of that long list

Phineas T. Barnum.

of travellers who have explored the wilder portions of every continent in the interests of my firm.

The first lot of animals which Cassanova brought us from Nubia arrived in the July of the following year, and consisted of two elephants, several young lions, and a number of hyænas, panthers, antelopes, gazelles and ostriches. It will be seen from this that during the decade which had elapsed since the purchase of the little menagerie at Bremerhaven—quite an important event to us in its time—the scope of our business had considerably enlarged. The demand for wild beasts was continually growing, Zoological Gardens were springing up on all sides, and public interest in exotic animals was stimu_ lated by the circuses and travelling menageries, which were now becoming numerous both in Europe and in America. Although we now began to send out travellers to all parts of the world—adventurous men who frequently explored regions where no European had ever been before—it was sometimes impossible for me to satisfy all the demands which I received. For instance, one of my chief customers was Phineas T. Barnum, the famous American circus owner. Barnum paid us his first visit in November, 1872, and on that occasion purchased animals from us to the value of about £3,000. He was touring Europe, he told me, in search of new ideas, and as I was able to supply him with some such (among other things I told him about the racing elephants of India, and of the use of ostriches as saddle animals) he paid me the compliment of inviting me to join him in his enterprise, with a one-third share of the profits. I preferred, however, to remain in Hamburg and develop my own business. After this, Barnum obtained his animals exclusively from me, and his successor, Mr. Bailey, continued this arrangement until 1907, when he disposed of his business.

The largest consignment of African animals which I ever received arrived in 1870. On Whit-Monday of that year I heard from Cassanova and from another of my travellers, by name Migoletti, that they were both making their way out of the interior of Nubia with huge caravans of captured animals,

and expected to arrive together at Suez.   Cassanova stated
that he was dangerously ill, and that it was therefore imperative
that I should come to Suez, in order to take charge of the
animals on the journey to Europe.   Under the circumstances
this appeared to be unavoidable ; and so, the next day, accompanied by my youngest brother, I departed for Egypt.
We travelled *via* Trieste, and arrived at our destination after
an uneventful journey lasting eight days.   On entering the
station at Suez we were greeted by some of our prospective
pets, for in another train opposite we saw several elephants
and giraffes, who pushed out their heads to welcome us.
This, however, scarcely prepared us for what met our gaze
when we reached the Suez Hotel.   I shall never forget the
sight which the courtyard presented.   Elephants, giraffes,
antelopes and buffalo were tethered to the palms ; sixteen
great ostriches were strolling about loose ; and in addition
there were no fewer than sixty large cages containing a
rhinoceros, lions, panthers, cheetahs, hyænas, jackals, civets,
caracals, monkeys, and many kinds of birds.

It was naturally no easy matter to transport this immense
collection of wild beasts to Europe.   The amount of food
required was enormous.   Besides the hay, bread, and sundry
other vegetable foods which were needed for the elephants
and other herbivores, we also took along with us about a
hundred nanny-goats in order to provide the young giraffes
and other baby animals with milk.   When these goats were
no longer able to supply us with milk they were slaughtered
and given to the young carnivores to devour.

The journey to Alexandria, where we were to embark
for Trieste, was by no means uneventful.   On the way to
the station the ostriches escaped, and were only recovered
after considerable delay.   Then one of the railway trucks
caught fire, endangering the entire menagerie ; and finally
we were furnished for the last part of the journey with a
drunken engine-driver who nearly burst his boiler.   Moreover, the poor creatures were so closely packed together that

it was impossible to feed them.   We travelled all through
the night, and arrived in Alexandria at 6 A.M.   Here
we joined forces with Migoletti's caravan.   The whole of
the next day was occupied in feeding and in general attend-
ance upon my unfortunate beasts, which had suffered considerably from their long train journey.   Thus it was not
until the evening that I was able to visit Cassanova, who

Embarking an elephant.

had preceded me to Alexandria.   Much to my regret I
found him sinking rapidly, and during the following night the
poor man died.   There was no time to mourn, however, for
on the next day the steamer was to be loaded with the living
cargo.   It will be readily believed that I suffered no little
anxiety when I saw my valuable animals, cumbrous elephants
and long-legged giraffes, hanging from the crane betwixt sky
and sea.   However, at last they were all safely deposited on
deck, and the passage to Trieste was accomplished without

serious mishap. Our arrival at that port caused great excitement among the townsfolk. And small wonder! No such collection of wild beasts had ever before been seen in Europe. The united caravans of Cassanova and Migoletti included, apart from the smaller creatures, five elephants, fourteen giraffes, four Nubian buffaloes, a rhinoceros, twelve antelopes and gazelles, two wart-hogs, four aard-varks, and no fewer than sixty carnivores. Among the latter there were seven young lions, eight panthers and cheetahs, thirty hyænas, and many smaller representatives of the cat tribe. There were also twenty-six ostriches, of which sixteen were full-grown birds. One of these, a female, was the largest specimen I have ever seen. This hen could easily reach a cabbage which I placed eleven feet from the ground.

Pretty nearly the whole population of Trieste must have turned out to watch us unload. And whenever an elephant or a giraffe came sprawling across in the crane a roar of delight would go up from the multitude on shore. It was truly marvellous that we ever reached the railway station without an accident, for the crowd in the streets was enormous, and we had the greatest possible difficulty in making our way through. We travelled to Hamburg *via* Vienna, Dresden and Berlin, and as some of our possessions found new homes in the Zoological Gardens in each of those cities, our numbers were greatly reduced by the time we finally arrived at our destination. This, as I have said, was the largest collection of the African fauna that I have ever received. It had been preceded, however, by several other successful expeditions (under the command of Cassanova and others) to the same region, and in a later chapter I shall describe the methods adopted for capturing the animals, and the difficulties which the expeditions had to overcome during the arduous marches out of the interior of Nubia.

At this time I was doing a roaring trade in African wild beasts, and splendid prices were paid for my wares, especially for elephants. I recollect one occasion when I sold three young elephants to an American animal dealer for the sum of £1,000. The reader may think that I had made a good bargain in this, and at the time I was under a like impression. But it seems I was wrong. For my American friend took the animals across to his own country and sold them for £1,700, £1,600 and £1,500 respectively.

I was married in March, 1871, and am blessed with five children and thirteen grandchildren, my two sons now being partners with me in the business. With the growth of the trade during the sixties and early seventies it became imperative to find a larger site for my menagerie; in spite of extensions, we had completely outgrown our old quarters in Spielbudenplatz. After a long search I found a suitable

Reindeer.

spot at Neuer Pferdemarkt, in Hamburg. This consisted of a dwelling-house, having a large garden behind—nearly two acres in extent—in which it would be possible to erect the necessary buildings, stables, etc. I therefore bought the place, and in April, 1874, we took up our abode in our new home.

The transference of the menagerie to Neuer Pferdemarkt brings us to the end of the first period in the history of the business. Hitherto we had been merely animal dealers; henceforth we were to initiate and develop other, though related, branches of trade. About the middle of the seventies the supply of wild beasts began to exceed the demand,

and the profits on my business somewhat decreased.   Some
remedy for this state of affairs had to be found, and the said
remedy eventually came through the chance suggestion of a
friend.   In 1874 I happened to be importing some reindeer,
and my friend, Heinrich Leutemann, the animal painter,
remarked that it would be most picturesque if I could import
a family of Lapps along with them.   This seemed to me a
brilliant idea, and I therefore at once gave orders that my
reindeer were to be accompanied by their native masters.

The Lapps, conducted by a Norwegian, arrived at Hamburg in the middle of September, and Leutemann and myself
went on board to welcome the little expedition.   The first
glance sufficed to convince me that the experiment would
prove a success.   Here was a truly interesting sight.   On
deck three little men dressed in skins were walking about
among the deer, and down below we found to our great
delight a mother with a tiny infant in her arms and a dainty
little maiden about four years old, standing shyly by her
side.   Our guests, it is true, would not have shone in a
beauty show, but they were so wholly unsophisticated and
so totally unspoiled by civilisation that they seemed like
beings from another world.   I felt sure that the little
strangers would arouse great interest in Germany.

The reindeer and the Lapps were safely disembarked,
but on the way up to Neuer Pferdemarkt a rather fortunate
accident occurred.   The deer were, of course, unaccustomed
to crowds, and two of them took fright and galloped away
through the town, finally taking refuge—not inappropriately
—in the Zoological Gardens.   My Lappic exhibition could
scarcely have had a better advertisement than was afforded
by this escapade.

My optimistic expectations were fully realised; this first
of my ethnographic exhibitions was from every point of view
a huge success.   I attribute this mainly to the simplicity
with which the whole thing was organised, and to the complete absence of all vulgar accessories.   There was nothing
in the way of a performance.   The Laplanders themselves

Laplanders.

had no conception of the commercial side of the venture, and knew nothing of exhibitions. They were merely paying a short visit to the hustling civilisation which they saw around them, and it never occurred to them to alter their own primi. tive habits of life. The result was that they behaved just as though they were in their native land, and the interest and value of the exhibition were therefore greatly enhanced. They took up their abode in the grounds behind my house at Neuer Pferdemarkt, and lived entirely out of doors. All Hamburg came to see this genuine " Lapland in miniature".

The Lapps, as is well known, inhabit the north of Nor. way, Sweden and Russia, and, in accordance with their occupations, are divided into the Fishing-, Forest-, and Up-land-Lapps. The latter are the least civilised of the three divisions, and it was to them that my little party belonged. They consist of tribes of primitive nomads, almost wholly dependent upon the reindeer for their subsistence. As I have already mentioned, they could not be described as beautiful. Their skin was a dirty yellow colour, their heads very round, their hair black, nose small and flat, and their eyes set somewhat obliquely. On the other hand their limbs were very finely moulded, and only Eskimos have smaller hands and feet than the Lapps. They reached a height of from four and a quarter to five and a quarter feet. It was most interesting to see the little people at work. They would set up and strike their tents as in their own country. No great labour is involved in this performance; their tents consist of poles covered over in summer with canvas and in winter with tanned hides, a hole being left at the top for the smoke to pass through. The Fishing- and the Forest-Lapps have become to a great extent Europeanised, for in-stance, in the matter of dress. But not so our little friends. They supply all their own needs, and by means of sinews they sew together the tanned hides of deer in a most dexter-ous manner. They make all their own snowshoes, sledges, etc. Men and women were dressed much alike, both sexes

wearing long skin coats, pointed fur caps and leather shoes.
It was most interesting to watch them catching the deer with
lassoes, and to see the wonderful skill with which they drove
their sledges.　The reindeer is verily their all in all, and takes
the place of cattle, sheep, horse and dogs.　The milking of the
deer was one of the chief attractions in this Lappic exhibition.
Our visitors were unspoiled children of Nature, and they no
doubt wondered what we could see in their simple household
goods, and in themselves, to arouse so much curiosity.

My experience with the Laplanders taught me that
ethnographic exhibitions would prove lucrative; and no
sooner had my little friends departed than I followed up
their visit by that of other wild men.　Our next guests came
from the Sudan—as was only natural, having regard to the
extensive intercourse I then had with that region.　The
attractions of this Nubian caravan were greatly increased by
the number of domestic animals which the people brought
with them, their great black dromedaries, for instance, arous-
ing much interest among the visitors to my Gardens.

Being desirous of carrying on my new anthropological
enterprise all the year round—in winter, as well as in summer
—I bethought me of the Eskimos, those dwellers in the
Arctic of whom we had all heard so much in connection
with polar expeditions, but who had never yet been seen in
the heart of Europe.　It might be possible, I thought, to
bring a small party of these people to Hamburg, where they
would indubitably cause a great sensation.　In the spring of
1877, therefore, I engaged a young Norwegian, by name
Adrian Jacobsen, and despatched him to Greenland for the
purpose of inducing a few Eskimos to accompany him back
to Europe.　The Danish Government were most obliging,
and not only at once gave their permission, but also conveyed
Jacobsen to their Arctic colony in a State steamer.　They
voyaged up the west coast of Greenland for a considerable
distance to a bay known as Jacobshavn, in lat. 69°.　Here
my traveller succeeded in persuading half a dozen natives to

pay a visit to the land of white men. The party was composed of a family of four persons, and two young bachelors.
The paterfamilias, a gentleman of about thirty, rejoicing in
the name of Ukubak, not
only brought with him his
obedient spouse and his
two little daughters, but
also the totality of his
worldly goods. These
consisted of dogs, sledges,
tents, weapons, household
implements, two canoes,
and so forth. The Green-
land Eskimos, who have
been well described by
Nansen, are more ad-
vanced in civilisation than
their kindred of the Far
North, these latter being
in an extremely primitive
stage of evolution, being
unacquainted even with
the " Kayaks," or canoes,
which play such a promi-

Ukubak and his family.

nent part in the life of the South Greenland natives. The
Greenlanders are, of course, under the protection of the Danish
Government, and they have adopted the Christian religion.
Nevertheless, their mode of life is not really very different
from that of their ancestors when Greenland was first recolon-
ised by the Scandinavians in the eighteenth century. They
have not been greatly altered through contact with Europeans.
They are still expert and enthusiastic hunters, pursuing with
great zest the numerous species of seals which inhabit the
Arctic regions. For this purpose they make use of curious
and highly characteristic boats, which they term " Kayaks ".
The kayak is a canoe constructed of skins, and is completely

decked over except for a small hole amidships. The canoeman, who propels his little vessel with a double-bladed
paddle, sits himself in this hole, which he exactly fits and
completely fills up, his legs being hidden beneath the foreward
decking.    In this position the Eskimos are able to execute
a most remarkable manœuvre.    If the canoe be upset, the
man is, of course, still firmly fixed in his hole, and is then
hanging head downwards from the upturned boat.    But so
skilful are they that, when this accident occurs and they find
themselves immersed, they are able by means of the paddle to
right the canoe and in this way save themselves from drown-
ing.    As may be well imagined, the ability to perform this feat

Ukubak's wife.

is an absolute necessity to
the Greenlanders in their
native haunts, for in rough
weather the small kayaks
are naturally very liable
to capsize, and any one
who is less adept than his
fellows will pay the penalty
with his life.    Ukubak
was a wonderfully expert
canoeman, and used fre-
quently to upset and then
right his kayak for the
edification of the visitors
to my Gardens.    He re-
garded it as a joke, and
never grew tired of re-
peating the performance.
The proceeding did not
even cause him any dis-
comfort, for, like all his
race, he was dressed in
waterproof clothing which, as I have said, completely filled

Devi -dancers' from Ceylon.

the hole and thereby prevented the water from leaking into the boat.

Ukubak was a man of moderate stature and prepossessing countenance. His better-half, too, was far from ugly, even from the European's standpoint. She was above the middle height, her figure was slim and elegant, and she dressed her hair most tastefully in a tower on the crown of her head. The Greenlanders made themselves at home on the spot where the Lapps had sojourned three years earlier, and built themselves a hut after the true Eskimo fashion, namely, half underground. I should perhaps mention incidentally that the Lapps are not, as might be supposed, close relatives of the Eskimos.

After the little party had been exhibited in Hamburg I took them to Paris, Berlin and Dresden. In Berlin the Emperor William I. came to see them and was greatly interested in Ukubak's aquatic tricks. On that occasion Ukubak remained so long under the water that the Emperor became quite alarmed for his safety, until I told His Majesty the facility with which the Eskimo could always recover himself when he so desired. In April of the following year, 1878, the Eskimos returned to their native land, greatly enriched by their travels.

From this time onwards I organised frequent ethnographic exhibitions, and I now have some show of this kind every year in my Zoological Park at Stellingen. Lapps, Nubians, and Eskimos have been followed by Somalis, Indians, Kalmucks, Cingalese, Patagonians, Hottentots and so forth. Towards the end of the seventies, especially in 1879, the animal trade itself was in an exceedingly bad way, so that the anthropological side of my business became more and more important. The outbreak of the war with the Mahdi, which occurred at about this time, closed what had hitherto been our chief source of supply, viz., the Sudan ; for it was now death to any European who was intrepid enough to enter that country. Even when the war was over, and the co-operating British and Egyptian Governments reopened the country, the

Sudan was found to have lost its glory, for the destruction of

A king and his two wives.

animal life in the interval had been terrible. · But more of this anon. The end of the year 1880 brought me some relief from my financial anxiety. My faithful friend Barnum sent me huge orders for elephants. Barnum and another American named Forepaugh were at this time strenuous competitors in the circus world, and the American public seem to have had an especial predilection for elephants. At all events, elephants were the chief attraction, and the fact was

very fortunate for me. The only difficulty was to find enough of the quadrupeds. I therefore sent one of my most famous travellers, Joseph Menges, to Ceylon in order to ascertain the prices of elephants in that island, and to find out whether large numbers of the creatures could be obtained there. Menges' reports were most satisfactory, and before long both he and certain other of my travellers were hard at work exporting a continuous stream of elephants from Ceylon. I was perpetually receiving fresh orders not only from Barnum but also from Forepaugh, for the rivals were continually endeavouring to overtrump each other

Joseph Menges.

Indian dancing girls.

in this matter, and in the year 1883 I exported from Ceylon no fewer than sixty-seven elephants.

In this place I ought to say a few words about Joseph Menges. He assuredly deserves a short biographical notice in this history of my business, for of all the fellow-workers with whom it has been my fate to labour, none has been more able and efficient. When this traveller joined my firm in 1876 he had already had considerable experience as an explorer. In the early seventies he had gone up the White Nile with Gordon, and few, if any, Europeans knew the Sudan better than he. He had become intimately acquainted with the peoples, the geography, the fauna and the flora of Nubia. He was, moreover, thoroughly accustomed to the climate. In those regions Europeans almost invariably suffer severely from fever, but Menges seems to have been immune—at all events, by the time he began to travel in my interests. On one occasion he brought to Europe for one of my ethnographic exhibitions some representatives of the famous Nubian tribe, the Hamran hunters, of whose manners and customs I shall have much to relate in Chapter III. Then he paid a visit to Somaliland, where he explored a district where no white man had hitherto been, and discovered a new race of wild ass. He succeeded in transporting to Europe a living specimen of this quadruped. Menges continued to lead hunting expeditions on my behalf until quite recently, and at the moment of writing there are still animals in my menagerie which have come into my possession through the energy of this trusty friend.

One of the largest of all my ethnographic exhibitions was the great Cingalese exhibition of 1884. This great caravan, which consisted of sixty-seven persons with twenty-five elephants and a multitude of cattle of various breeds, caused a great sensation in Europe. I travelled about with this show all over Germany and Austria, and made a very good thing out of it.

When this Cingalese exhibition had come to an end

I thought the public might, perhaps, have had enough of ethnology for the time being, and I therefore set to work to devise some new form of entertainment. The result of my meditations was a revolution in the methods of training wild beasts for the circus. For many years, indeed ever

Patagonian.

since I could remember, I had been greatly distressed at the cruel methods of teaching animals to perform, which were then in vogue. My enthusiasm for my own calling originated more, if I may say so, in a love for all living creatures than in any mere commercial instincts. I had no doubt inherited this passion from my father, and under the circumstances in which I found myself there was, of course, every opportunity of cultivating the taste. I do not intend to imply that I have not also had an eye to the main chance; but I can, I think, say with perfect truth that I am, and always have been, a naturalist first and a trader afterwards. This being the case, it was only natural that I, in common I am sure with all other lovers of animals, should be greatly distressed at the wicked ill-treatment to which "tamed" beasts were in those days subjected. In a later chapter I shall relate some tales about this barbarous method of training—now happily a thing of the past—and I will only say here that the poor brutes were driven to perform their "tricks" by being thrashed with whips and burned with red-hot irons.

For many years I had been pondering over this subject,

and I had come to the conclusion that the prevalent mode of procedure was not only cruel, but also stupid and ineffectual. Brutes, after all, are beings akin to ourselves. Their minds are formed on the same plan as our minds; the differences are differences of degree only, not of kind. They will repay cruelty with hatred, and kindness with trust. What, there-fore, could be more foolish than the senseless manner in which every spark of intelligence was driven out of the hapless pupils? I knew full well from long and intimate association with the lower animals that their understanding develops wonderfully by close friendship with man, and I was convinced that far more could be achieved by gentleness and sympathy than was ever accomplished by tyrannical cruelty. This, however, was not my only discovery. I had also found from experience that animals of the same species differed most remarkably in character, and from this I inferred that if the talents of each animal were to be fully developed, individual tuition during training would be absolutely essential. Here again we have a point of similarity to ourselves. These, then, were my ideas upon this not unimportant subject, and about twenty years ago I proceeded to put them into practice.

I established a circus in Hamburg in 1887, and before long I found a trainer whom I induced to adopt my new methods of educating the animals. I met this man (whose name was Deyer-ling) in England, and as he happened to be unemployed I engaged him on the un-derstanding that he should work on my system only. I at first showed him what

Hagenbeck's first circus.

I proposed to do by training dogs and cats to perform tricks without ever resorting to force (except in cases of gross disobedience), and I then expressed to him my opinion that if this could be done with these small carnivores, a like result could be achieved with lions and tigers.

The first experiment in this "gentle" training, as I will call it, was made with lions during the years 1887-89. For my purpose I used no fewer than twenty-one lions, but so variable are the characters of animals, that only four turned out to have the necessary talent for the work. I will not go into details of the training in this place, but will only say that the success with the remaining four lions was nothing short of astounding. They carried out all manner of tricks, the climax of the performance coming when the trainer harnessed three of the mighty carnivores to a chariot and drove triumphantly around the cage. This troupe first appeared in the Nouveau Cirque in Paris in 1889, and during the next few years they were exhibited in many other towns, bringing me, I may mention incidentally, a very large profit.

At that time all the world was looking forward to the great exhibition at Chicago, which was to take place in 1893, and it occurred to me that it would be a grand thing if I could exhibit there a huge troupe of performing animals, trained on my new humane system. I therefore commenced to get together a large collection of wild beasts for this purpose. My troupe consisted of twelve lions, two tigers, several cheetahs and three bears. These performers were first exhibited in 1891, at the Crystal Palace, in London, where they were in charge of my brother-in-law, Heinrich Mehrmann, who in the meantime had become my most distinguished animal tamer. At the Crystal Palace they were an immense success, and two Americans offered me 50,000 dollars for the troupe—a handsome sum. This offer I refused, little knowing that I was thereby throwing £10,000 into the gutter.

I was now in for a bad time. One day in September I heard from Mehrmann that the animals were sick, and that he was unable to diagnose the ailment. As the beasts were to be brought back to Hamburg in October, and as the trouble did not sound serious, I thought it unnecessary to take any

Somalis.

steps until after I had been able to inspect them on their
return home.   So nothing was done.   When, however, a few
weeks later, the animals arrived in Germany, we discovered
to   our   dismay that they were all suffering from glanders.   In
spite of our care, the disease proved fatal in every case ; all
the creatures either died or had to be put out of their misery.
The cause of the illness seems to have been the bad meat
which was supplied by the unscrupulous contractor in England.

Here was a pretty mess !   All the hopes I had founded
upon the now famous achievements of my magnificent troupe

Fuegian family.

were in the space of a few days dashed to the ground.   Yet
I was only at the beginning of my troubles.   I set to work to
make up new troupes, but death, though in a different form,
overtook these also.   During the first part of 1892 numberless
inmates of my menagerie were seized with an extraordinary
illness.   They began by being afflicted with vomiting and
diarrhœa, and later fell into convulsions, usually dying within
a few days.   Both young animals and adults were attacked
by this inexplicable ailment, though the latter for the most
part recovered.   The most expert veterinary authorities were
as completely mystified as myself.   Only later did the correct
explanation of this grievous pestilence become clear.   In

3 *

August the cholera broke out in Hamburg. Now my pets had perished with all the symptoms of cholera, and if the correct diagnosis had occurred to us, it is conceivable that the dire disaster which overtook Hamburg that autumn might have been prevented. It would seem that the delicate constitutions of the exotic animals were very susceptible to this plague, for, as I have explained, the cholera attacked the beasts for some months before any human beings suffered from its ravages. How true it is that cholera is spread through the agency of foul drinking water, was clearly demonstrated by the fact that after the veterinary surgeon had ordered the animals to be given boiled water only, no more of them were attacked by the disease.

In spite of these great losses I still had a few animals left which I hoped to exhibit at Chicago. Then a further difficulty arose. One day towards the end of 1892 I suddenly received a cablegram from a gentleman who was my partner in this American enterprise, in which I was informed that I must send my animals over to England immediately, for if I failed to do this the United States Government would not permit me to bring them to Chicago in the following year. The American authorities feared that the beasts might spread the cholera in the United States, and they insisted upon this period of quarantine in England. To England therefore the whole collection went, regardless of expense, and there the creatures sojourned for the whole of that winter. Luckily for me, the British Government did not meddle in the affair, and raised no objection to England being utilised as an asylum for the beasts. Next year the menagerie was shipped across the Atlantic and duly established in Chicago. Just before the opening of the exhibition, Mehrmann fell ill, and I was compelled to put the chief troupe of performing animals through their tricks myself, although I had had nothing to do with them for five months previously. However, the show went off quite well.

Since that time I have sent out many troupes of perform-

ing animals into all parts of the world, notably to the great
exhibition of St. Louis in 1904, and all these are trained on
my own humane system, which is, indeed, now adopted by
all respectable animal tamers.   In my park at Stellingen, the
establishment of which I am about to describe in the next
chapter, an excellent troupe of lions and polar bears is to be
seen.   These are in charge of the expert trainer Fritz
Schilling, who appears in the accompanying photograph.

Schilling with lion-tiger hybrids.

# CHAPTER II.

## MY PARK AT STELLINGEN.

In the previous chapter I have related the earlier history of my business. I still have to give a record of its subsequent development into the great animal park now existing at Stellingen.

As the years rolled by, my business gradually increased until its branches extended to all parts of the world. To its original purpose, *viz.*, the buying and selling of live animals, many new purposes came to be added. I had ethnographic exhibitions; I was interested in the propaganda of the new humane method of training wild animals; I had breeding experiments; and there were many other ideas which I was only awaiting an opportunity to carry out. For the execution of all these projects the space now at my disposal was wholly insufficient. It became therefore a matter of the first importance to acquire an extensive tract of country, where I should be free from the handicap of a confined space. Especially was this necessary for my experiments in acclimatisation. These it had now become essential for me to undertake, seeing that a large portion of my business was in the importation of game from foreign countries for sporting purposes, and trading in the many kinds of domesticated animals. I was, moreover, receiving orders to supply animals for the new Zoological Gardens which were springing up in Morocco, China, Japan, Argentina and elsewhere. This alone required a good deal of room, and a removal had clearly become a necessity.

I found, much to my regret, that my additional requirements could not be met in my native town of Hamburg. I had indeed acquired in 1888 an additional piece of ground in that city larger than my grounds at Neuer Pferdemarkt, but it was not large enough ; and the neighbouring lands, which all belonged to the State, were withheld from me in the most rigid manner by the authorities. I was thus driven to look elsewhere. It so happened that I was one day recounting my troubles to a friend living at Stellingen, a place in Prussia not very far from Hamburg. Scarcely had I finished speaking, than my friend took me by the arm and led me to a hedge opposite his house over which he showed me a piece of land having an area of about four and a half acres, which he said was to be had very cheap. I lost no time in settling the matter. Within two days the land was my property. Immediately afterwards I found that two neighbouring estates were to be sold, and within twenty-four hours these also had passed into my possession.

Thus it was that I became the owner, after years of searching, of a splendid estate on elevated ground, admirably suited to the foundation of a park for wild animals. Plans were drawn, and men set to work without delay, and in five months' time twelve large enclosures and five animal houses were ready to receive their inmates.

Although the locality which I had selected was in itself admirably suited to the purpose that I had in view, it had the defect of being somewhat distant from the remainder of my establishment in Hamburg. The communication between Hamburg and Stellingen also was bad; and I set to work to consider the possibility of buying up more country between the two places, and of establishing a direct means of communication between them. In this way the area of my animal park would have scope for unlimited expansion as the business grew, and I should be in no danger of being shut in, as I was at Hamburg. The undertaking was a large one, and I had to find other capitalists to co-operate with me. This, after some delay, I succeeded in doing. Two brothers contributed each £5,000. I myself put in £7,500 and gave an undertaking to transfer my establishment completely to Stellingen.

Now at last I was in a position to carry out my long-nursed project of founding a Zoological Park of a totally different kind from anything that had been before attempted. I need not here go into the details of my plan : they will appear in subsequent chapters. I will content myself with stating the fundamental principle. I desired, above all things, to give the animals the maximum of liberty. I wished to

Framework of artificial mountains.

exhibit them not as captives, confined within narrow spaces, and looked at between bars, but as free to wander from place to place within as large limits as possible, and with no bars to obstruct the view and serve as a reminder of the captivity. I wished also to show what could be accomplished in the way of acclimatisation. I desired to refute the prevailing notion that luxurious and expensive houses with complicated heating apparatus were necessary for keeping wild animals alive and healthy. I hoped to show that far better results could be obtained when they were kept in the fresh air and allowed to grow accustomed to the climate. I wished my new park to be a great and enduring example of the benefits that can be wrought by giving the animals as much freedom and placing them in as natural an environment as possible. A certain point must be fixed in the garden from which might be seen every kind of animal moving about in apparent freedom and in an environment which bore a close resemblance to its own native haunts.

For the chamois, the wild sheep, and the ibex, artificial mountains had to be thrown up; for animals of the plains, wide commons had to be set apart. For the carnivores, glens had to be established, not confined within railings, but separated from the public only by deep trenches, large enough to prevent the animals from getting out, but not in any way interfering with the view. In the midst there must be a central building with a large arena for performing purposes; while, close by, it was necessary to establish large areas for accommodating animals who were not permanent residents but only there in transit. Of these I now have a very large number. Whereas ten years ago I scarcely sold twenty head of game for sporting purposes, I now sell many hundreds yearly. In old days I considered that I had done well if I sold six or eight camels in a year. I now think little of selling one hundred. In zebras, also, my trade has grown from three or four specimens a year to fifty specimens. All these animals have to be housed while in transit. Seeing that the trade in many other kinds of animals has increased in a similar proportion, it is obvious that a very large area is needed for this purpose. Even among elephants, which I used to keep up to the number of twenty in my old establishment at Neuer Pferdemarkt, the numbers are now greatly increased, and in 1904 I had no less than forty-three of these great creatures at the same time.

The work of transforming this virgin land into a pleasure park was immense. From its original waste condition it had to be altered in a great variety of ways. Mountains had to be thrown up, and valleys and streams had to be dug out. Stables and luxurious buildings also had to be erected. Moreover, as opportunity afforded, I was continually adding to the extent of my territory ; and by watching for occasions of picking up neighbouring estates at a cheap price, I gradually increased the area of my park. I succeeded after considerable difficulty in selling my land in Hamburg, some of it to the Hamburger Vereinsbank, and the remainder to the State, after having overcome every difficulty put in my way by the worthy Town Councillors of Hamburg. Thus at last we were finally planted at Stellingen.

The acquisition of the land and the remainder of the preliminary preparations were completed in October, 1902, and in that month we were able to commence operations in transforming the land and building the houses, etc. The estate itself consisted at first of nothing but wide fields upon which grew half a dozen trees. To carry out my plans no

less than 40,000 cubic metres of earth had to be shifted, before the surface of the land alone was prepared. A large army of workmen were turned on to the job, and day by day I saw the work develop, as one after another of the ideas, which I had so long dreamt of, were realised before my eyes. At last on 7th May, 1907, the opening ceremony took place—the crowning triumph of many years of strenuous labour.

Since the establishment of this great park my business has continued to increase without intermission. As an instance of the large scale on which my trading transactions are conducted I may mention that in 1906 I supplied no fewer than 2,000 dromedaries to South West Africa for the German Government. In the variety as well as in the magnitude of my business development has taken place. Many experiments have been carried out in housing animals and acclimatisation ; in breeding and the crossing of different

Entrance to the animal-park a Stellingen.

races with one another ; and finally, in the course of the last year I succeeded in the final achievement of establishing an ostrich farm.   Since my park is a wholly new kind of menagerie it has, of course, attracted much attention, and I have received visits from various distinguished persons, including one or two from the German Emperor himself.

# CHAPTER III.

## HOW WILD ANIMALS ARE CAUGHT.

I MUST now proceed to describe the manner in which the various denizens of my animal park are captured in their native haunts, and must relate, in particular, the interesting experiences which my travellers have had in the Sudan, in Rhodesia, and elsewhere.

There is no business or profession in existence in which the science of travel, and all the difficulties connected therewith, play such a prominent part as in the animal trade. In the exercise of his business the animal trader has to search the uttermost parts of the earth. In the primeval forests of Africa, in the deep jungles of India and Ceylon, on the vast steppes of Mongolia and Siberia, the traveller wanders for weeks, nay for months at a time, in search of the strange dwellers in the wild.

Unlike the hunter, who is attracted only by the love of sport, the animal trader goes to work. He goes, not to destroy his game, but to take it alive ; and consequently not the least of the difficulties with which he is beset is the discovery of some practicable way of bringing back his booty to civilisation. As a rule, every foot of the arduous journey is attained only at the expense of some loss to the caravan.

Books and maps dealing with the countries where we carry on our work are few and far between, for naturally the localities where wild animals are to be caught are very remote from all the more civilised parts of the world. Nor are these the only obstacles ; for uncivilised peoples, no less wild than the beasts, have to be secured and made friends with—a matter of no small difficulty.   Moreover, travellers' tales about wonderful animals which are to be caught—but which never yet have been caught—send many expeditions upon fruitless errands.

The Egyptian Sudan is one of the richest and most inexhaustible sources of animal life.   This region is of enormous extent.   One of those best acquainted with it, my old friend and faithful fellow-worker, Joseph Menges, the world-wide traveller, speaking of it, says : " Speaking widely, one can include in this area the whole of the North Abyssinian plain, which stretches from Massowah to the upper Blue Nile. The main hunting region consists, however, of the district of Taka, beginning in the east with the upper Chor Baraka, and ending in the west with the upper courses of the Rahad, a tributary of the Blue Nile."
This country consists largely of steppes, interspersed with bush, from which rise picturesque rocky hills, which in Abyssinia begin to assume the character of wild highlands.   The fauna of the country is wonderfully rich : the African elephant, the black rhinoceros, the hippopotamus, the giraffe, the lion, the panther, the hyæna, the

At work.

hyæna-dog, the aard-wolf, the jackal, wild-asses, the Kaffir-buffalo, and many kinds of antelopes ; also the wart-hog, the aard-vark, the porcupine, baboons, and other monkeys.   The avifauna is also very rich : the swift-footed ostrich, the marabou, the secretary-bird, various kinds of vultures, the rhinoceros-hornbill, francolins and others.   Crocodiles, snakes, etc., make up the list of animals which can be hunted in this fruit ful district.

It is only natural that this wealth of fine animals, including most of the giants of the animal kingdom, should for a long time have attracted the attention of Europeans ; and the region may be described as one of the classical countries for capturing animals.

For many years this animal paradise was closed, and the angel with the flaming sword who guarded the gate was Abdullahi Kalifat el Mahdi, the false follower of a false prophet. None of the animals inhabiting the country could be brought to Europe ; and for this reason, that to meet with the Mahdi meant both for Europeans and for Egyptians almost certain death, or at the very least long captivity. Nevertheless it would be a mistake to suppose that these regions are inhabited by a fanatical, bloodthirsty population ; for the savage barbarity which prevailed was entirely confined to the rulers. Although the country is so rich in game, the inhabitants are for the most part not hunters ; much more often they are either resident peasants, eking out their livelihood by the additional pursuit of some trade in the country villages near by ; or else nomads, leading their herds from pasture to pasture and carrying their tents and household goods upon the backs of their camels.

In spite of their peaceable disposition, such of the Nubians who do adopt the pursuit make bold huntsmen. For people born in a land so richly stocked with game, hunting is the most natural of callings. On the banks of the rivers, in the almost impenetrable forests, and on the plains, which in the rainy season are covered by grass ten to fifteen feet high, the elephant wanders in herds of from fifty to a hundred head, the black double-horned rhinoceros feeds in pairs, and gentle giraffes, wild Kaffir-buffaloes, and fleet antelopes are to be found in hundreds. And the great carnivores follow in their tracks. The native hunter knows the favourite resorts of his quarry, and follows their trail with those remarkable powers of tracking which characterise savages. He pits his cunning against the timidity of the animals. Entire families and villages devote themselves to the dangerous but attractive occupation of hunting, and in this way regular hunting castes have been built up.

4

The most eminent of these castes is that of the sword-hunters or "Agaghir," who consider themselves the aristocracy of their profession; and not without reason, for the method of hunting adopted by them, and which is almost peculiar to Taka, needs courage, activity and skill.

The method of the sword-hunter is peculiar, and, with certain kinds of game, dangerous. In all cases the object of the huntsman is to sever the Achilles tendon of his quarry. Where giraffes, antelopes, ostriches or similar harmless creatures are concerned, the sport calls for no greater skill than is required to ride over uneven and treacherous ground. But where rhinoceros, lions or elephants are being pursued, the case is different; and it then often happens that the positions of hunter and hunted are reversed. The ponies used for this purpose are of Abyssinian breed; and, like their riders, they are small, strong and fiery.

On the whole, the most dangerous game to hunt with the sword are elephants. The chase is usually carried out by a band of four or five experienced men, united by so strong a bond of fellow-feeling that, when the life of any one is in danger, each of the others will unhesitatingly risk his own in attempting a rescue. Menges, who is an old hand at this work, describes the course of events somewhat as follows: The streams and drinking-places are first searched for signs of elephant-trails. When once these are hit upon, they are followed up till the great beast is reached. This is no easy matter, for the African elephant is a great wanderer, travelling often for a whole day and night without a halt. More frequently, however, the herd wanders during the cooler part of the day through the forest and steppes, and stops to rest during the hotter hours of noon. At this time the herd is usually very compact, and almost invisible in the thick foliage; so that the chances of a successful assault are small. The most suitable moment for attack is when the herd is much scattered; it is then comparatively easy to select a bull with good tusks and isolate him from the rest. Once isolated, his first impulse

4 *

is flight; but the huntsmen surround him, and no loophole of escape remains. Then with a loud trumpeting, which strikes terror into the breasts of the unfortunate ponies, he launches himself furiously against the nearest of his enemies.

Now it is generally arranged that all the huntsmen should be mounted on dark-coloured ponies, with the exception of one, who rides a grey. The attention of the elephant, whose sight is not good, is attracted by the colour. Upon the grey pony, therefore, the mighty creature usually directs his attack. It is the business of the rider, at the first onset, to turn and flee. The elephant promptly gives chase; and the flying huntsman, ignoring the fact that the slightest slip means death, endeavours to keep just out of reach, though near enough to hold the animal's attention concentrated upon him. In the meantime his comrades follow the elephant from behind, and whoever reaches him first springs from his pony, and delivers a dexterous blow with his sword on the left hind leg of the animal, which cuts the Achilles tendon, and lames him on one side. As the elephant hastily turns to avenge himself upon this new enemy, it becomes the turn of the rider who was formerly being chased to stop, dismount, and with a similar blow on the right hind leg to lame the animal on the other side, so that he is totally disabled. If the blows have been delivered with sufficient skill and force, the arteries of the hind legs have been cut, and the elephant bleeds slowly but almost painlessly to death. If there is a gun at hand, his sufferings are more quickly terminated. Once he is dead, hours of arduous labour commence. The tusks are broken off; the hide also is removed, to be used for shields or sword-scabbards, or for harness for ploughs. The flesh is left for vultures and wild beasts, unless, indeed, there should happen to be in the vicinity a camp of the nomads. In that case the carcase is appropriated by them. They cut the meat into strips and dry it in the sun (like the South American *charqui*); it is then put aside for use in the rainy season.

For the European, armed with weapons both accurate

and deadly, big-game hunting is attended with little danger. In the Arctic Regions the polar bear, once so formidable, now excites scarcely more fear than the musk-ox; while in Africa the sportsman approaches to within a few paces of lions or elephants, to photograph them before he despatches them. But for the natives big-game hunting is a very different matter. Then the fray is far from one-sided; the weapons of the man are little, if at all, superior to those of the brute; and the "hunting" is more of the nature of a hand-to-hand encounter, requiring the utmost skill and courage on the part of the human combatant. Should a horse stumble—an accident which, on that uneven ground, intersected by underground streams, is only too likely to happen—death either to the animal or its rider is the probable result. We need not be surprised that the Sudanese assert that the professional elephant-hunter never dies at home, but ends sooner or later under the tusks and feet of a hunted elephant.

The rhinoceros, buffalo and lion are also killed by swordsmen in the same way as elephants. The giraffe, antelope and ostrich are chased until fatigue overcomes them. In their case, although there is no danger, the strain both upon man and horse is severe, on account of the length and swiftness of the pursuit. We might go at much greater length into the mode of killing wild animals in this interesting country, from the skilful ostrich-hunting of the Bedouins, to the wholesale slaughter of the European "sportsman". Our special concern, however, is not with the killing of animals, but with the methods of catching them alive; let us therefore follow the career of one of my hunters, who has been sent on this errand.

Daybreak at Atbara. A gentle breeze stirs the grassy steppes; the trees are suffused with the bright glare of a rising African sun. In the thick woods on either side of the river there is the twittering of countless swarms of birds, from the gigantic marabou to the little swallow which flits over the

water. Away in the distance there rises from the glassy
water the uncouth head of a crocodile—or is it only a sand-
bank? It is already becoming hot, and the air is humming
with myriads of insects. In our station, situated not far from
the river-bank, life is beginning to stir.

The enclosure or seriba in which our station is settled is
surrounded by a large fence made of branches of trees, and
has only one entrance, which is carefully stopped by thorn
branches. Within the enclosure are huts, built of straw, for
the Europeans and their black servants, as also stalls for the
animals that are captured, and some stores of food-supply.
The fires which were lighted in various parts of the seriba to
frighten away wild animals have long ago gone out, and now
the working-day is about to begin in earnest.

My hunters had arrived only the day before, and everything was pleasure and excitement. The whites, who knew
the language, greeted their black friends with heartfelt
warmth ; and on both sides presents were liberally exchanged.
Those given by the blacks consisted of fatted sheep, fowls,
eggs, honey and other forms of delicacies, which the whites
amply repaid by goods dear to the black man's heart. So a
great feast had to take place, at which such of the presents as
were edible were eaten—for the most part by the donors
themselves. This was followed by war-dances and sham-
fights with lances, swords and shields, accompanied by drums
and shrieks ; while the women indulged in graceful group-
dances, amid much clapping of hands and beating of drums.
Camel- and horse-racing were the most important items of the
entertainment ; and conviviality was carried far into the night,
by the light of the laager fire.

By the next morning everything has settled down, and
business commences in earnest. Crowds of curious natives
collect around the camp, many of them in search of employment as hunters. Hunting cavalcades are engaged, receive
their directions, are equipped with arms and ammunition, and
sent off in various directions.

Came transport (South-West Africa).

The method which these cavalcades generally pursue in the capture of young animals is to chase the herd, until the young, lagging behind, can be isolated from their parents. They are then easily seized and made secure. Among giraffes and antelopes this procedure is attended with but little danger; and even among buffaloes, which have no qualms about deserting their young, the work is compara_tively safe. But in the case of rhinoceros and elephants, for which the demand is much greater, the capture is not so simple. These great creatures turn vigorously to defend their young; and the latter cannot as a rule be secured without first killing the old ones. This is done by the swordsmen of Taka in the manner already described. The catching of young giraffes by the expedient of chasing the herds until the young can no longer keep up was first practised in Kordofan during the thirties of last century. I need hardly mention that the utmost care has to be taken of the captured animals. A herd of goats is taken along, in order to keep up a constant supply of fresh milk; but even with this precaution a large number of the captives die soon after they have been made prisoners, and scarcely half of them arrive safely in Europe.

The Takruris—Mohammedan negroes who have emigrated from Darfur—are especially skilful in hunting and trapping. They are equally adept in catching hyænas, panthers and baboons in carefully constructed traps, or in digging out porcupines, or in securing birds, such as secretary-birds, francolins, etc., in snares and nets of ingenious patterns. This versatility renders them invaluable to us as assistants.

The Havati, or water-hunters, carry on a very specialised trade. Their particular quarry is crocodiles and hippopotami; and, being very expert swimmers, they actually attack these creatures in their own element. The weapon employed is the harpoon. A long cord is attached to it, so that the harpoon, after it has been cast, can be drawn back again by the thrower. The time usually selected for this sport is the hot hours of noon, when the crocodiles are lazily sunning

themselves on the sand-banks, and the hippopotami are floating
dreamily at the surface of the water. Once the animal has
been harpooned, it is surrounded by swimmers and pushed
ashore, where it is quickly despatched by lances. When it is
desired to take the beasts alive a slight variation on this
procedure is adopted. The young, of course, are alone
selected; and the harpoons are hurled so as to inflict as small
a wound as possible. With constant attention this will probably soon heal up. Although this mode of harpooning calls
for much skill and experience, no less than three-quarters of
the hippopotami formerly brought to Europe used to be caught
in this fashion.

If one is to believe the comic journals, all that has to be
done to catch a lion is to throw a bag of pepper in his face,
and then proceed to chain him up in safety. To catch a
monkey they suggest that one need only leave a pair of
boots, well smeared with lime, in the grass, when the creature
will come of his own accord and pull them on, and remain
stuck fast till the hunter arrives to take him home. Very
different from these facile methods is the reality.

In one of our regular hunting-grounds, in the neighbourhood of the Mareb or Gash, lives the great brown baboon,
known as the Atbara baboon (*Cynocephalus doguera*). The
rugged and barren rocks of this picturesque region resound
with the cries and grunts of these baboons, who wander about
in herds of a hundred or more. They often come down for
food to the palm-woods which border the banks of the river,
or pay a highly unwelcome visit to the natives' doura[1]
plantations. Our station here was situated on the Gash, a
rain-stream which contains water during the rainy season,
while during the rest of the year its course is marked by a
streak of glistening sand. Our camp lay just beneath the
Sahanei mountains, and close to a great cluster of rocks which
swarmed with baboons. Here and there pools of water were

---

[1] A kind of corn, *Sorghum vulgare*.

left in the dry river-bed, in places where the subsoil prevented
the water from trickling away; and close to our station were
several such pools which the baboons used as drinking-places.
All day long we used to hear them fighting and chattering as
they came to drink, and even by night there was little quiet.
On the narrow ledge of rock above the pools whole families
—or perhaps I should say harems—used to collect. We
could hear plainly the low grunts and squeaks with which the
mother lulls her baby to rest; we could hear the grumbling of
the father, who has been disturbed by the noise. Suddenly
there would be a yell; and thereupon the whole herd would
break into frantic screaming. The baboon's arch-enemy, the
slinking panther, has tried to make an assault. It was impossible to help admiring the fine old males, full of courage
and self-reliance. It was to make their nearer acquaintance that we had come here; and since they were not sufficiently versed in European politeness to accept an invitation,
more active measures must be taken to secure their attend-
ance.

In the success of these more active measures we were
greatly aided by the arrival at our station of our old friend
Abdulla Okutt—a member of the half-savage tribe of Basas
and a well-known ostrich-hunter. All the apparatus required
consisted of cords and a few axes, together with a number
of assistants, who of course expected to be liberally rewarded with "backsheesh" for each animal captured. Ah!
poor monkeys, look out for yourselves now; the mighty
Abdulla is on your tracks!

The first thing to be done was to stop up all the drinking-
pools, save one, with thorn-bushes. The baboons were thus
all compelled to use this one. They took to it the more
readily, in that, the whole time we were there, we had been
careful not to interfere with or frighten them in any way, so that
they were quite unsuspicious of any trap. We encouraged
them still further by scattering doura about the pool—a proceeding which was so much appreciated that the older

animals would often keep away the young until they had devoured it.

When, by these treacherous means, thorough confidence had been established with the baboons, the time came for setting the traps, which were to make them still more our guests, and eventually also emigrants. The trap is a fairly simple contrivance. The base is circular, about two and a half yards in diameter, and is composed of tough rods twisted together. Round the outer edge of this base, at intervals of about a foot, are fixed stout stakes, leaning inwards so as to meet together at the top. The framework thus constructed is interlaced with branches of trees, tied together with cord; and the whole structure then makes a solid cage, of considerable weight, and somewhat resembling a native's hut in appearance. When it has been completed it has to be conveyed to its proper situation in the neighbourhood of the drinking-pool. Here one side of it is left open, being propped up with a strong stick, and the baboons are gradually inveigled into it by leaving doura inside. When they have become thoroughly accustomed to the trap, the final stage in the proceedings commences. In the darkness of night a long cord is attached to the pole which holds the trap open. It is carried along, buried loosely in the sand, until the other end reaches a hiding-place, whence a good view of the cage can be obtained. Then comes the tragedy. A blazing noonday sun drives the thirsty baboons chattering down to their drinking-hole. Some of the biggest males, who have already secured a monopoly of the doura, enter the trap, and commence their feast. The hunter awaits his opportunity: it soon comes; a tug on the cord, the trap closes with a bang, and three great baboons are fairly caught.

Then there follows a scene, both comical and painful, which baffles description. For a moment the astounded prisoners sit benumbed with terror and unable to move; then they anxiously begin to seek an exit. The herd outside, no less surprised, flee at the first alarm; but they soon return and congregate round the trap, urging the captives with ear-splitting yells and grunts to find their way out. Some of the boldest jump right on to the top of the trap, and appear to carry on an excited conversation with their friends inside. At least that is what the American Professor Garner would say, who, by dint of much imagination and little science, has for years past been laboriously constructing a monkey-language.

The hunters, however, cannot afford to wait while this scene is going on, for baboons are endowed with great strength, and would soon break through the walls of their cage. On the approach of their captors they show all the signs of extreme terror, and endeavour to force their heads through the walls. And now, as may easily be imagined, comes the really critical and dangerous part of the performance, namely, to take the animals out of the cage and secure them. The hunters are provided with long stakes, forked at the end, which they push through the branches forming the cage-wall. With the forked ends they catch the baboon's neck, and pin him to the ground. When all the baboons have been thus secured the upper part of the cage is removed, and the creatures are firmly bound. First their jaws are muzzled with strong cord, made of palm-strips; then hands and feet are tied; and lastly, to make assurance doubly sure, the animal's whole body is wrapped up in cloth, so that the captive has the appearance of a great smoked sausage! The parcel is then suspended from a pole carried by two persons, and conveyed triumphantly to the station.

These great baboons have strong nerves—no wonder, they neither smoke, drink, nor do any work, and always live in the fresh summer air! So, after a brief period of exhaustion, followed by a day or two of quiet, they recover their normal spirits. The large males must, however, be carefully watched. They are very angry and jealous, and will probably kill any other of their kind put in to keep them company. Even females are likely to have a poor time of it; for the males keep all the food to themselves, and allow their women to go

hungry.    It is on account of the selfishness of the males that
females and young baboons are so rarely caught in the cages
by means of bait.    When by chance one does get in, it is
usually allowed to escape again.

Menges, who has worked much on these baboon-stations,
and whose account I here follow, has a low opinion of the
intelligence of the animals.    This he has derived from the
circumstance that the same individual, when allowed to
escape, is so often caught again in the same trap.    There is no
doubt that this is the case ; and, since the traps are large and
easily recognisable, it seems to argue no great intelligence on the
part of the creatures.    Abdulla relates how he caught one young
female, which he could recognise by a scar on the mouth, no
less than three times—each time, I regret to say, with a different husband.    On the third occasion he gave her a good
hiding with his sjambok, and sent her about her business.
But another explanation of their falling so frequently into the
same trap is possible.    For, among baboons, domestic discipline is very severe ; a female has to do exactly what her
husband wants, or else there is a row.    In the case mentioned
above it is very probable that the female, having been twice
widowed and then appropriated by a third husband, was
compelled to follow him, however unwillingly, into the trap.

However entertaining baboon-catching may be to read
about, it is a very serious business for the actors.    The
beasts have very powerful teeth and prodigious muscular
strength ; and if one of them should happen to escape, he
might inflict severe injury upon his captors.

Our station soon fills up with our four-handed guests.    In
eight days we have caught no less than twenty-two of them,
all from the rocky wastes lying near the camp.    They take
kindly to their captivity, however ; and, from the very first
day, have taken the food provided for them.    Their comrades, still at large, do not forget them ; and often after the
midday drink will come close up to the seriba, and, climbing
up the tall palm-trees, howl out unintelligible words, which

are answered with mournful voices by the prisoners within. What a real tragedy for these poor baboons! The conversation finally degenerates into an ear-splitting chorus. On one occasion a baboon, bolder than the rest, jumped the thorn barrier of the seriba and dashed up to one of the cages, in which, maybe, he saw his brother, or father, or uncle sitting. But he was speedily driven away by the attendants, amidst the most appalling yells from the herd watching outside.

Sometimes baboon-catching is a much more sanguinary business than this, especially in the case of the large silver-grey "Tartarin" or "Arabian baboon" (*Cynocephalus hamadryas*). This is a very pugnacious species, and, moving as it always does in large herds, very dangerous to encounter. One of my younger travellers tells a story of a baboon-fight in Abyssinia, in which nearly three thousand baboons took part. They are certainly very savage animals to look at. When fighting they erect their manes and show their teeth and strike the ground furiously with their hands, as they advance to within a few feet of their enemy.

The capture of these "Arabian baboons" differs very little from that already described. A trap is put out at the drinking-pool in the same way as before; but, instead of having one trap-door, it has two, one on each side. The use of this second door is as follows: On arriving at the trap one baboon chief stands at the door to guard it, while only a few are admitted within. But those that are excluded slink round to the back; and, finding another entrance there, the cage soon fills. Then, as before, the cord is pulled, the trap closes, and a terrified cry breaks from a thousand throats. It was on such an occasion as this that the fight, already alluded to, and in which 3,000 baboons joined, took place. The whole army hurled themselves savagely upon the hunters, who defended themselves as best they could with firearms and cudgels. They were driven back, however, by sheer force of numbers; and the victorious baboons made short work of the cage and released their imprisoned friends.

Many touching scenes were witnessed in this battle. One little baboon, who had been injured by a blow from a cudgel,

Hagenbeck coming !

was picked up and safely carried off by a great male from the very midst of the enemy. In another instance, a female, who already had one infant on her back, picked up and went off with another whose mother had been shot.

It is not often, however, that the hunters fail in their task, as on this occasion. When once the animals are enclosed in the trap their fate is sealed. The method of removing them from the trap is somewhat different from that already de_ scribed. The old ones are shot; a small hole is then cut in the side of the trap, and to this is applied the mouth of a small cage. However they may clamber about the walls of the trap, the baboons inside are at last compelled to enter these small cages, in which they are safely carried off.

The natives catch baboons in the same way as other animals, namely, by pursuing them, when they come down into the plains to rob the doura fields, until they are thoroughly worn out. The young ones, and the mothers carrying babies, lag behind the rest, and are then easily isolated and secured.

To return to the seriba at Atbara. The day of our de- parture is drawing near. The stalls and yard are filled with captive animals—young elephants, giraffes, hippopotami, and buffalo. Our primitive wooden cages are also well stocked with panthers, pigs, and baboons; so that the first part of our work—that of catching the animals—is completed. But now comes the second part, which is attended with even greater difficulty than the first, namely, the transport of the animals across the desert to the port of embarkation on the Red Sea. In order that the transport may be successful it has to be organised with the most detailed thoroughness and foresight. The work before us is that of conveying across the waterless desert a party consisting of 150 head of cattle and over 100 heavily-laden camels, together with the whole menagerie of captured animals. Ours, however, is a very orderly caravan, as it creeps along in the silence of the night, like a great snake, across the wide expanse of glistening sands. The moonlight throws long shadows behind the dunes; and the solitude is only broken now and again by the wild laugh of a

hyæna.  The night is usually chosen for travelling, on account of the comparative coolness which is then enjoyed.  In
the daytime all the countries surrounding the Red Sea are
scorched with heat, the thermometer often rising nearly to 45°
C. (113° F.) in the shade.  At night, although the temperature
does not fall so very much, yet one does at least enjoy immunity from the fierce glare of the sunlight.  Of the two
fundamental difficulties of travelling, the great heat and the
scarcity of water, the former is overcome by journeying only
at night, and the latter by careful preparations.

The caravan commences its march shortly before sunset ;
each man falling into his proper position at the appointed
time.  The larger animals are driven along by one or more
attendants—a giraffe taking three persons, an elephant from
two to four, an antelope two, and an ostrich, if large, also two.
The smaller animals, such as young lions, panthers, baboons,
pigs or birds, are carried in cages roughly constructed on the
spot ; and these cages are placed on the backs of camels.
Right in the midst of our procession there marches a group of
camels harnessed in pairs.  Over the pack-saddles of each
pair are laid two stout poles, and from these poles, between
the two animals, hangs a large cage, made of strong rods
bound together with strips of hide.  Each cage contains a
young hippopotamus, who, in spite of his youth, weighs with
his cage well over a quarter of a ton.  Each of these distinguished travellers requires a large party to wait upon him ;
for, in addition to the two camels which convey him along,
six or eight others are required for carrying the water which
he demands continuously throughout the journey, as also
for the bath — made of tanned ox-hide — which he enjoys
every day during the long halt.  Hundreds of head of
sheep and goats are driven along with the procession ; the
nanny-goats providing a constant supply of milk for the
young animals, and the remainder being used as food for
the carnivores.

The speed of the caravan, being the speed of the slow-

est animal, is not great.    We march during the earlier part
of the night ; then there is a halt to feed and water the
animals ; after which we push on again till about an hour
after sunrise.    During the day we get what protection we can
from the fierce rays of the sun, by sheltering under mimosas
and acacias, or by making a rough covering of mats.    The
drinking-places in the desert are few and far between ; and,
when we come upon one of these welcome oases, a special
day of rest is granted.    But even then it is not always easy
to take possession of them.    For they are often occupied by
nomad tribes, who are only too ready to resort to arms in defence of them, and can only be appeased by a liberal use of
"backsheesh".    The drinking-places are often as much as
sixty miles apart ; and since this means a three- or four-day
journey for our slow-moving caravan, it may easily be imagined how great a quantity of water has to be carried with
us.    It is kept in leather bottles made of goat- or ox-hide ;
and so precious is this fluid, upon which hang all our lives,
that it is difficult to think that it is nothing more remarkable
than plain water.

However carefully we organise our expedition, it is
inevitable that many of our captives should succumb before
we reach our journey's end.    The terrible heat kills even
those animals whose natural home is in the country.    The
powerful male baboons are very liable to sunstroke, which
kills them in half an hour ; and any weak point in their constitution is sure to become aggravated during the journey.
Whether this is due to the terror and strain which they under-
went at their capture, or to being confined in cramped cages,
I cannot say.    But the fact remains that not more than half
of them arrive safely at their destination, despite our utmost
care.

The long anxiety of these weary journeys is seldom wholly
unrelieved by amusing incidents.    One such incident occurred
one day as we were passing through a valley in Northern
Abyssinia.    As the caravan was drawing up at a well,

5 *

it fell in with an immense herd of " Arabian " baboons, whose grunting and yelling drew answering cries from our captive baboons. We were soon surrounded by these great monkeys ; and even when we resumed our march they refused to leave us, running along on either side of us, keeping up an incessant conversation with their imprisoned relatives. Now and again one would advance to within twenty paces of the cages, and

Disembarking a camel.

Disembarking an elephant.

with violent gesticulation and screaming would seem to be adjuring the captives to break loose and come to join them. But these brave champions of liberty soon had to retire before the volleys of stones hurled at them by our camel-drivers ; and after a time they disappeared in the darkness of the night.

At last the laborious journey, which has lasted from five to six weeks, comes to an end ; and the caravan, or such of it as still remains, reaches the port of embarkation on the Red Sea. The motley crew take up a camping-ground close to the town, to await the arrival of one of the steamers, which periodically call there, to take them to Suez. At Suez they are either transhipped to a steamer coming from India or the Far East; or preferably they are sent by train to Alexandria, and shipped from there to one of the Mediterranean ports—Trieste, Genoa, or Marseilles. When they arrive there another railway journey still lies before them, and it is usually another ten days before the animals and their keepers are safely lodged at Hamburg. The entire journey from the camp at Atbara or on the Gash occupies nearly three months.

During the long period of the Mahdi's régime, when the whole country was closed, many changes were wrought in this paradise of animals. Under the joint government of Egypt and Great Britain order has been slowly restored, but alas! the country is not what it was. There is scarcely a tenth of the game now that there was thirty years ago. The elephants, formerly so abundant, are only found in small herds; the rhinoceros is almost extinct; the giraffe is rare; antelopes have altogether vanished from many localities · while thousands of buffalo have fallen victims to the rinderpest.

The war against the Mahdi is both the direct and indirect cause of this sad destruction of animal life. When the Egyptian Government was overthrown, the natives came into possession of large stores of modern breech-loaders; which, in the intervals between killing each other, they used for killing animals of all kinds. It must be admitted that they had a strong incentive to this slaughter. For, while the treasury of the Mahdi was filled to bursting, the people of his kingdom were being decimated by starvation. When the Sudan had been utterly ravaged, and nothing was left to plunder, the wild game was the only means of sustenance that remained to them; and a fierce rush for meat took place. Whole armies set up their camps in the midst of our hunting-ground and slaughtered game *en masse;* especially the Baggara-Arabs of the White Nile, hunters no less famous than the swordsmen of the Taka district. The Abyssinians, too, who suffered under the same fate as their Sudanese neighbours, were driven to the same extremes. Their favourite quarry was the elephant ; and they not only took the tusks, but devoured the flesh, not even rejecting the tough meat of the legs. On one occasion a border prince organised a regular elephant drive, at which no less than fifty-six of the animals were slain in a single day. On this occasion the scene of action resembled a pitched battle, for twenty Abyssinians were left dead on the field ; most of them, it is true, killed, not by the elephants, but by aberrant bullets from the rifles of their own friends.

In Abyssinia driving is a favourite method of attacking game. The number of men available is unlimited, and all living creatures are regarded as imperial property ; so that there are no obstacles in the way of this pursuit. A zebra-hunt, in which one of my travellers took part, may be described as an example of the way in which these drives are carried out. An army of as many as 2,000 soldiers form a circle enclosing a very large tract of country, where the zebras are known to be. The locality is selected so that near the centre of the circle there passes one of the dried-up river-beds, so common in that country. These sandy river-beds are flanked on either side by high rocky banks. The large circle of men begins to contract, driving the zebras into the centre. The animals spring lightly into the river-bed, from which they are unable to escape, by reason of the steep sides. A guard is set in the river-bed on either side of them, so as to prevent their moving up or down. When they are thus securely penned in, a barbarous spectacle takes place. A thousand soldiers attack the zebras with long whips, and thrash them for hours, until they are thoroughly exhausted, and their spirit tamed. This manœuvre is attended with much danger, and on the occasion in question thirty-three men were either killed or severely wounded during the fray.

The animals are then fettered, and driven off to the huts of
the natives.    There they are fastened up, by ropes attached
to each of the
four legs, and
tied to pegs.   In
a few days' time
they become
quiet and can
soon be driven
about, without
any necessity for
taking precau-
tionary mea-
sures.    Grévy's
zebra, the species
of which I am
here writing, is

Captured zebras in the kraal.
(German East Africa).

easily domesticated.    It has, moreover, a strong constitution
which would fit it well for the service of man in more civilised
countries.    The Kilimanjaro zebra, on the other hand, is
a difficult animal to tame ; in its stubbornness it is very like
a donkey.

In the Sudan, at the end of the Mahdi's régime, we found
the country changed, not only in respect of the game, but
also in respect of the people who used to be our friends and
assistants.    Misfortunes had so overwhelmed them that the
famous tribe of Hamran, from which all the best sword-
hunters were derived, was reduced to twenty men.    Sword-
hunting itself was no longer practised, and was known to the
younger generation only through the tales of their parents.
The Havati or water-hunters also were no more.    Both
these methods of killing game had been superseded by the
more effective, if less exciting, rifle of modern times.

The capture of young animals is effected in other ways
besides that of chasing them until they are overcome with
fatigue.    Traps of various kinds are used ; and in the case of

young hippopotami pitfalls are very commonly employed. The success of this method is due to the habit of the hippopotamus of allowing its young to trot along in front of it, instead of behind, so that it can keep a look-out for any danger which may threaten its young one. The pitfall is made in a track which the animal is in the habit of using, and is covered over with branches to conceal it. As the hippopotamus goes along with its young one in front, the latter suddenly seems to vanish into the earth ; and the terrified mother, though not wanting in maternal affection, is so taken aback that she turns and flies, leaving her offspring to its fate. Then, if all goes well, the hunter secures his booty without further trouble. On one occasion, after a young hippopotamus had been caught in this fashion, the natives came rushing into our camp beaming with joy, shouting to us " Bana kiboko makufa ! " (The hippopotamus is dead). Nothing was left to us but to reply "Nakula kiboko!" (Eat it up) ; for it was their anticipation of this permission that had caused all the rejoicing and tumult. It often happens, when the animal is left a night in the pit, that it is found by a lion ; and in the morning nothing is left of it but skin and bones. But when no mishap has occurred it is still a matter of some little difficulty to extract the hippopotamus from the pit. A palisade is first erected round the mouth of the pit ; and over this palisade a noose is thrown round the neck of the animal. When these creatures are agitated they break into profuse perspiration, which causes them to become so slimy and slippery that it is difficult to make the noose hold. For this reason, it is passed not over the neck only, but over the forelegs as well. As soon as the noose is fixed in position the animal is hoisted a few inches off the ground, by the combined efforts of about twenty men pulling on the rope. Half a dozen others jump into the pit, and bind together the forelegs and the hindlegs, as also the jaws ; for the animals are obstinate and malicious, and it does not do to run any risks with them. Unlike the rhinoceros, which soon learns to know its keeper and will follow the caravan like a

dog, the hippopotamus is an animal to be treated with caution.
When the captive has been made fast the palisade is broken
away, and a sloping path is dug out of the pit to the surface of
the ground. A
litter is made of
stout poles and
branches, the hip-
popotamus is laid
upon the litter and
secured there with
more branches
twisted together ;
and he is then
hauled out. The
most laborious
part of the work
now commences,
namely, the trans-
port through
swamp or forest
to the nearest
river A road
has to be hewn
the whole way
through the bush.
Arrived at the
river, he is placed
upon a native
barge ; but before
being embarked

Kalmuck priest.

for Europe he is accustomed to captivity and to the food
supplied him. The difficulty of carrying him may be inferred
from the fact that the young animal may weigh as much as
half a ton.

Some of the most arduous, as well as the most expensive,

of the expeditions which I equipped and sent out, were those
to Mongolia and Siberia. Especially interesting was one
despatched at the instigation of the Duke of Bedford for the
purpose of catching and bringing home to Europe some
specimens of the wild horse (*Equus prjwalsky*). Attempts
had often been made before to secure this animal, but, with
one exception, they had all miscarried. This exception was
in the case of the famous naturalist Falz-Fein, who had
brought some individuals of this rare species from the steppes
of Asia to his estate in the Crimea. Little, therefore, was
known about the wild horse; its distribution, its habits, the
best mode of capturing it were still unstudied. The conduct
of the expedition was entrusted to Wilhelm Grieger, one of
my most reliable travellers. On him fell the responsibility
of making the preparations for the journey, and afterwards of
leading the expedition into Mongolia. He was provided with
plenty of money, and also letters of introduction and safe-
conduct from the Russian Government, the Chinese Am-
bassador in Berlin, and Prince Alexander of Oldenburg.
This latter one was of particular value in procuring a warm
welcome from the eminent Buddhist Lama, Dr. Radmai,
then resident in St. Petersburg, who placed at the disposal
of the expedition his great knowledge both of the people and
the country of Mongolia.

The first thing to be done, however, was to pay a visit
to Falz-Fein in South Russia, in order to ascertain from
him where these wild horses were to be found. This Grieger
did; but he found Falz-Fein reluctant to divulge the information he required. By indirect means, however, Grieger succeeded in ascertaining that the horses were to be found in the
neighbourhood of Kobdo, a town situated under the northern
slopes of the Altai Mountains—a very long journey right
through Russia, and Western Siberia, into Mongolia.

Having procured this information, Grieger returned in
high spirits to St. Petersburg, whence the expedition was
to set out. But at the last moment another obstacle was

A Ka muck caravan.

encountered, which delayed the start several weeks.    Dr. Radmai pointed out that the current coin of Europe was quite useless on such a journey.    The medium of exchange in most request consists of large flat silver pieces weighing about 12 lbs. each ; and it was necessary to have a large quantity of these manufactured at Hamburg before starting off.    The metal is much lighter in colour than ordinary English silver ; and for small purchases it was the habit to break off portions of the coin of whatever size might be required. Tea and coloured woollen bands were also of use as money in Mongolia.

Soon after the arrival of the money in St. Petersburg, Grieger set forth upon his journey, full of hope for a successful issue to his adventure.    The time selected was winter— a typical Russian winter, with town and country covered deep in snow.    This inclement season was chosen, in order that the arrival in Mongolia might take place in the spring, when the young foals had just been born ; and also that the severity of a Mongolian winter might be avoided.    It is true that Mongolian summers bring their troubles, as well as the winters.    The climate there is typically continental ; that is to say, the temperature fluctuates with great rapidity and through extreme variations.    Thus it may not infrequently happen that 80° F. (27° C.) is registered during the daytime, while there is a frost at night.    The cold nights, however, do little to destroy the insect pests which afflict the traveller in the warmer season.    The banks of the Kobdo River swarm with myriads of tiny gnats which settle in clouds upon the horses when they go to drink.    They attack in particular the tender underparts of the animal ; and exposure to their bites for half an hour is sufficient to ruin them effectually : death ensuing from loss of blood and from inflammation.

Grieger, who took with him only one assistant, travelled by the Siberian Railway through Moscow as far as Ob, where the line is crossed by the river of that name.    From there he journeyed southwards by sledge about 170 miles to Biisk, a

place some fifty miles from Altai.    Up to this point the
journey had been performed with comparative ease.    Scanty
provisions could be obtained at the widely separated stations
which they passed on their way ; but from Biisk the real
difficulties of the expedition commenced.    Native drivers and
riders were hired for transporting into the interior the tents,
provisions, money, and other baggage belonging to the

Mongolian village.

travellers.    Riding on horses or camels, through deep snow
and in intense cold, 600 miles had to be traversed to reach
Kobdo by way of Kaschagatsch.    On one occasion when
the thermometer fell to 50° below zero (F.) the fifty cases
of sterilised milk which had been taken as food for the
captured animals froze hard.

Although Kobdo had been selected as the headquarters
of the various expeditions, there was little in that distant
town that could be of any use to the travellers.    The town

itself has about 1,500 inhabitants, three-quarters of whom are Mohammedan Tartars belonging to a Turkestan tribe, while the rest are Chinese merchants, trading in the products of Mongolia. Besides the town itself, there is a fortress and a prison; and also the governor's palace, for it is a Government centre. Kobdo is the terminus of the great caravan route from Peking, which for camel caravans is distant a two and a half months' journey.

A Kalmuck national dance.

The country north of the Altai Range is not wholly un-inhabited. Along the banks of the river Zedzik-Noor there dwell various Mongolian tribes of nomadic habits, each governed by a chief or prince; and in his excursions from Kobdo, Grieger usually found them very friendly. He arrived at his destination some time before the foaling period had commenced, and filled up his time by studying the aborigines, enlisting assistants, and hunting. The hardships which he had to undergo at this time were often severe. He had nothing but a tent to live in; and with the temperature at 50° below zero it was impossible to keep warm even with blankets and furs. Often he had to go without a fire, owing to the difficulty of collecting fuel. The fuel generally used in the country is dried cattle- or horse-dung, which, when rubbed into powder in the hands, can easily be ignited with steel and tinder. The wind soon fans the spark into a flame; or, if there is no wind, the Mongolian will sit on his haunches and blow patiently away until there is a good fire. But the amount of dung available was often insufficient to meet the demands of the travellers.

Of food, on the other hand, they had no lack, though little variety could be obtained. For four months mutton was almost the only food; and with this they drank " Tsamba," a mixture of tea, butter and salt, which is universally esteemed throughout Mongolia and Tibet. Tsamba is made as follows : Tea is powdered in a wooden mortar, and is then poured with salt and butter into boiling water. The butter is obtained from the milk of sheep or goats. This is well mixed, boiled milk and salt are added; and the whole is then boiled once more. The beverage thus prepared is not so nasty but that one may soon become accustomed to it. Not so easy is it, however, to become accustomed to the Mongolian method of cleaning the drinking bowl before the liquid is poured into it. All he does is to spit into it, and then rub the bowl carefully round with a greasy corner of his coat. Another native drink is called Arka, and is prepared from the residue of milk that has been evaporated.

The Mongolians, as may well be surmised, are not fastidious in their choice of food. Indeed, they are prepared to eat anything whatever that comes in their way, except what is forbidden by their religion. They consider it wasteful to slaughter healthy cattle, when there are any weak or diseased to be had; and they have no qualms about eating an animal which has died a natural death. The intestines, even, after being drawn through the fingers to eject the contents, are thrown into the cooking-pot with the rest.

Expedition in search of Mongolian wild horses

The customs of the Mongolians are often curious and interesting. They have no system of burial, but merely throw out their dead on the steppes to be preyed upon by vultures, crows, and dogs. They are still in the pastoral condition, no agriculture being attempted. They are all mounted, and carry old-fashioned guns. Both men and women wear trousers of blue linen, and high boots, the soles of which are made of many layers of linen cloth, reaching a thickness of almost an inch. Tobacco is always in great demand among these people ; and their rank may be approximately judged by the quality of the pipe which they smoke. The tube of the pipe is made of wood, and is quite straight, a foot or more in length. The mouthpiece is adorned with an agate stone, the size and value of which is an index of the wealth and prominence of the possessor.

The district between Kobdo and Kara-Ussu is volcanic in origin, and is a plateau covered by short grass, and dotted with conical peaks. The valleys are often thickly wooded, and give rise to very pleasant scenery.

The Mongolian is hospitable but not communicative. A characteristic of their conversation is the constant repetition of the phrases which they use. The following is the sort of conversation we used to carry on with them :—

*Mongolian.* " Mendi " (God be with you).

*Traveller.* " Mendi."

*Mongolian.* " Malzuruk mendi baina? " (Are all your household well?).

*Traveller.* " Mendi baina."

*Mongolian.* " Tana del chabana? " (What are you doing here?).

*Traveller.* " Manna chuduludu gores " (I have come to buy wild animals).

The tents of the Mongolians are surrounded by very fierce jackal-like dogs ; but as soon as the owner sees a stranger approaching, he drives them off, and makes the visitor welcome. The traveller's horse he secures by knee-

6 *

haltering, and then drives out to pasture. At whatever
hour of day or night he may arrive, the housewife (or should
we say tentwife?) does all that can be done, in the preparation
of food and a couch, to make him comfortable.

At last spring came upon the land; the snow melted,
and the rivers ran free once more. Grieger soon discovered
that the Zedzik-Noor was simply full of trout, of a large and
palatable kind. So thick were they in the stream that they
could be taken out by pulling a large vessel through the
water; and one afternoon's catch exceeded a hundred fish.
These Grieger tried to cook by smoking over a fire; but the
first attempt was a failure, for the bodies fell into the fire, only
the heads remaining suspended from the hooks. But necessity is the mother of invention; and Grieger soon hit upon a
method of cooking them.

These operations were watched by the natives with horror
and disgust; for they class fish with snakes, and regard it as
an unclean food. This, no doubt, was the cause of the ex
traordinary abundance of trout in the river when Grieger
arrived. If the Mongolians shunned fish, they made up for
it by their eagerness to obtain meat, and Grieger's tent was
surrounded by idlers and beggars on the look-out for pickings.
To disperse these, who constituted a considerable nuisance,
Grieger hit upon a very original plan. He took a piece of
meat, and covered it thickly with pepper, an article of food
unknown to the nomads. He then handed it out to them;
and as soon as they began to eat it, such a spluttering and
sneezing took place that they hastily fled and did not trouble
him again. Sausages he made of lungs and livers, but these,
for some reason, the natives would not touch. Occasionally
hunting brought in supplies. The great wild sheep, the argali,
were an especial delicacy, the ten-year-old rams in particular.
Now and again onions were found. In the Kobdo valleys,
Grieger obtained a large collection of birds, including one
species of pheasant, hitherto unknown. Birds, known to the
natives as mountain- or rock-hens, were chased by the native

sportsmen, who ascertained their whereabouts by watching for the ravens which would soar above them in the sky. Grieger's shooting-parties sometimes disclosed an unexpected spirit of compassion in the natives. On one occasion, for instance, as he was passing some Mongolian huts, with his gun over his shoulder, one of the occupants came out, and besought him not to shoot hen-birds, as it was the breeding season. This anxiety arose, not from the sportsman's motive

The river Kobdo.

of keeping up the stock (for the Mongols themselves do not eat these game birds), but from a genuine pity for the hen-bird with her young.

During these minor diversions the main object of the expedition was kept constantly in mind. Grieger carefully cultivated the friendship of the chiefs; and through their means a hunting-party was gradually got together. The aborigines were wholly new to the idea of hunting animals for the purpose of capturing them alive. Their expeditions were undertaken solely in order to kill game for food ; and in all the proceedings which were taken they had to be instructed beforehand by the leader.   Since only young animals were wanted, watch had to be kept to ascertain when they had become fairly independent of their dams ; and it was found that the proper time for starting the hunt was during the first half of May.

Observation showed that there were no less than three varieties of the wild horse in the neighbourhood, closely resembling one another in form but showing differences of colour.   They all have wavy hair over the body and legs, and blackish eyes, while in the foals the colour is variable.   The wild horse wanders about in herds of twelve to fifteen ; but even in this district it is not very numerous.

As compared with the prolonged preparations which were necessary, the actual catching presented but little difficulty.   The method employed was that which has already been mentioned as being the usual method, when young animals only are to be caught.   It is a habit of the creatures to rest for some hours during the daytime in the vicinity of the drinking-place.   The Mongolians were instructed to seize this opportunity of stalking them with their own horses.   Then at a given signal the whole company break into shouts and yells ; and mounting their horses dash upon the herd.   The latter spring up in alarm and gallop off into the steppes, leaving behind them nothing but a cloud of dust. The Mongolians give chase, and after a time brown specks are seen at intervals in the dust-cloud.   As the chase continues the specks become larger and turn out to be the foals, which are unable to keep up with the older members of the herd.   When at last the foals are quite worn out, they stand still, their nostrils swelling and their flanks heaving with exhaustion and terror.   All the pursuers have then to do is to slip over their necks a noose attached to the end of a long pole, and conduct them back to camp.   Here there are in readiness a number of tame mares with sucking foals, which are requisitioned as wet-nurses for the new arrivals.    In three or four days the foster-parents and their young become quite friendly.

So easy did the Mongolians find this horse-hunting, when once they had been shown the way, that they went out to do some catching on their own account; and before long no less than thirty foals were secured in the camp.    This placed Grieger in some difficulty.    The order, which he had come to execute, was only for six.    Ought he, then, to incur the additional expense of bringing home thirty?    There was nothing for it but to telegraph home to find out.    His journey to the nearest telegraph office and back took him over more than a thousand miles of country, and involved him in an absence of three weeks from the camp.    When he arrived back, armed with permission to bring the lot, he found that the industrious Mongolians had increased the number to fifty-two.    With these the long journey home was commenced, the party consisting not only of the wild foals, but also of their foster-parents, the animals carrying the travellers and their baggage, and thirty native recruits. Slowly the caravan wound its way over hill and dale, in rain and sunshine, in heat and cold.    Anxiety for the safety of the captives was never absent.    Many of them, as was inevitable, died on the journey, in spite of all the care that could be exercised.    And in other ways the journey was decidedly eventful.

Wild horses.

Before many days were passed the first incident occurred, namely, the escape of the camels, owing to the carelessness of the attendants ; and it was only with great trouble that their recapture could be effected.   The attendants turned out to be a bad set; for after a few weeks Grieger noticed that they were becoming discontented.   At last a deputation approached him and announced the intention of the entire company to throw up the work and abandon the caravan, saying that the way was too long, the journey too difficult,

A herd of yaks.

and making many other similar excuses.   The money, paid them in advance, they would as conscientious men return. In vain did the traveller use all the arts of persuasion to induce the people to remain.   In vain did he point out to them that the caravan would be totally lost if they were to desert him at this moment.   At last the leaders of the mutiny professed themselves ready to remain, if a rise in salary were granted them.   As soon as Grieger discovered that the whole affair was merely a vulgar attempt at extortion, he changed his tactics.   Seizing his Kirghise whip, he promptly proceeded to distribute the augmentation of salary asked for, but in

heavy blows instead of coin! This treatment was immedi_
ately successful, the mutiny calmed down, the ringleaders
begged for pardon; and before long the caravan was jogging
merrily along again, without the desertion of a single man.
In all, the transportation to Hamburg took eleven months.
Out of the fifty-two wild horses which had started, twenty-
eight arrived safely at their journey's end, where they were
henceforth placed upon a diet of hulled oats, warm bran and
carrots. Thus ends the story of how wild horses first came
to Northern Europe.

Of all the countries traversed by the animal dealer, none
present such great difficulties as the vast plains and forests
of Siberia. The problem has still to be solved as to the
proper way of transporting wild sheep, ibex, roe, pheasants,
tigers, wild asses and other dwellers in this region to civilised countries. The distances which have to be traversed
are immense; and as a rule there are no roads at all to travel
on. Food for men and animals has to be carried by the party,
for it often cannot be obtained by the way; and half the
animals usually die in transit. A few years ago I equipped
another expedition, and sent it out to this Kobdo country, to
obtain some young specimens of the argali or giant wild
sheep. This I hoped to cross with the larger kinds of our
domesticated sheep, so as to obtain a breed of giant domestic
sheep which might be serviceable to farmers. The expedition
was unsuccessful; and another which I sent out soon after fared
no better. More than sixty of the animals were captured, but
lived only a short time. In the course of the journey home
every one of them died from diarrhœa. These two fruitless
expeditions cost no less than £5,000.

Of all the animals which the dealer endeavours to catch,
perhaps none are so easy or less dangerous than snakes. In
fact, snake-hunting might be better described as collecting
than hunting. In the great marshes of India, the so-called
Sundarbans, snakes are sought out during the cool season in the

early mornings by the natives, who are well acquainted with the haunts of the reptiles. Before dawn they are so benumbed with cold that they can easily be caught. This is done either by means of a net at the end of a long pole, or by a long forked stick, by which they can be fixed round the neck and pressed to the ground. In this position it is not difficult to make them secure. During the dry season another method is employed.

Argali (wild sheep).

Nets are laid out round a selected spot, which is then set on fire. The snakes, in their hurry to escape, become entangled in the nets; but this method can only be used for the large reptiles, as the smaller kinds would easily pass through the mesh. In snakes supplied to me from Calcutta I have often noticed marks of burning. But on these animals wounds soon heal up.

The great python of Borneo (*Python reticulatus*) is caught by the natives when it is torpid from the effects of a heavy meal.    It is then entangled in a large net thrown over it, and safely lodged in a bamboo basket.    For longer journeys, they are placed in large four-cornered boxes with holes bored for the admission of air.

The most remarkable way of finding snakes is that resorted to by the snake-finders of India, who discover them by the smell.    They go in the early morning, when the creatures are torpid, taking with them their baskets and ropes, and proceed to smell out their quarry, which are thereupon dug out of their holes and secured.    Many large species, including the python, are caught in this fashion.

In old times snake-charmers went everywhere, showing off in every circus or menagerie in Europe and America. At that time the snake trade was very lucrative, and I used to import them by the gross.    Once I received as many as 276 specimens in a single day, all belonging to the one species *Python bivitatus*, which sold largely in America. Snake-charmers now belong to the past, and there is little money to be made in the trade.

It is a far cry from the sweltering plains of India to the cold northern seas, but I hope I may be allowed to take this jump and describe the methods of capturing the common seal and other kinds of pinnipeds.    The work is comparatively simple. Advantage is taken of the fact that seals come out of the water by night to sleep on

Sea-lions in Peru.

the sand-banks.  Under cover of darkness the hunters creep

cautiously up to the sleeping-ground, and set long nets along
one side of it.   While this is being done a second party of men
go round in boats to the other side of the sand-bank, and there
await the signal that all is ready.   As soon as the signal is
given, this second party make for the sleeping seals with loud
shouts and gesticulations.   The terrified animals rush precipi-
tately towards the sea and soon become entangled in the nets.
Without delay net bags are thrown over the young individuals
to prevent their escaping.   These creatures have very sharp
teeth, and it is advisable for the hunters to wear stout
Wellington boots when engaged in this occupation.   I have
known as many as thirty caught in this way in a single drive.
Twenty of these were adults and soon died, but the rest were
young and thrived well in captivity.

Not the easiest part of the business is the transport of the
animals to Europe in the sealing ships.   The young seals are
kept in great water tanks, and it is sometimes difficult to get
them out when they have to be disembarked.   Seals have to
come to the surface of the water every few minutes for the
purpose of breathing, and one of these intervals is chosen as
an opportune moment to catch it either in a large landing net
or with a noose.   As so often happens among wild animals,
the older individuals are very morose and unmanageable.
They think of nothing but regaining their liberty, and cannot
be persuaded to take any food.   The young, on the contrary,
seem quite happy in their new surroundings and soon learn
all kinds of tricks.

To my mind there is no nobler kind of game than the
eland antelope.   Specimens of this animal first came into my
possession in a very curious manner, through the agency of
Dr. Carl Peters, the famous traveller.   After a long day's
march under a burning African sun he arrived at the farm of
a Boer in Rhodesia.   In the course of the evening they fell
to talking about the ravages which the tsetse-fly and the
rinderpest wrought among the cattle.   Dr. Peters had often

before been struck by the great difficulties to which the lack of draught animals subjected the farmers.   His present host had adopted a novel method of making good the deficiency. Seeing that domestic animals were impracticable, he proposed to catch the indigenous wild animals of the veldt and convert them into beasts of burden.   Now the wild game of Rhodesia, though sadly diminished in numbers in the last fifty years, is still fairly abundant.   If the herds are no longer to be num- bered in thousands, they may still be numbered in hundreds. Kudu, hartebeest, wildebeest, ostriches and eland antelopes are all plentifully distributed throughout the country ; and the Boer had selected the antelopes for breaking in as draught- animals.   As Dr. Peters showed interest in his scheme, he took him to a neighbouring enclosure where half a dozen fine elands were confined.   He explained to Dr. Peters that he hoped to be able to use them not only for ploughing, but also as carriage horses.   The traveller asked him at what price he would value these antelopes when their training had been con- cluded.   The Boer named a figure which, though certainly none too small, appeared to afford Peters some amusement. The latter produced from his pocket an English illustrated magazine with which he had beguiled the weary evenings for some days previously, and showed the Boer a number of pic- tures of Carl Hagenbeck's Institute at Hamburg.   "This man," said he, "will give more for the animals than they are worth to you ; why not sell them to him?"   The Boer adopted the suggestion on the spot and I suddenly received a telegram : " Have sixteen eland antelopes.   Offer them you so many thousand marks.   Wire decision and take over in Rhodesia within six weeks."   I closed with the offer at once, and sent my traveller Johannsen to Rhodesia to fetch them home.   Long delays often occur before animals can be trans- ported to their destination, but in the course of nine months he brought home not only the sixteen eland antelopes which I purchased from the Boer, but a number of others which he succeeded in catching by a device which he learnt from the

Boers and negroes in the neighbourhood. This device is, I think, sufficiently interesting to be worth recording. The preliminary operations are similar to those by which the Mongolian wild horses are captured. When a herd of elands has been found, about thirty mounted hunters surround them, and, stealing cautiously up, suddenly burst upon them from all sides. It would be a hopeless task to try to catch the adults, for an eland bull weighs over a ton and is much more powerful and fleet than any horse. They break into a furious gallop and soon vanish out of sight. But the young, with their ungainly stilt-like legs, are soon overtaken ; the hunter rides up to them and secures them by catching hold of their tails—a manœuvre which is often not very easy to carry out while on the gallop.

In order that the animal may be kept alive, when caught, various precautions have to be taken. The hindlegs are tethered, and the body is carefully wrapt up in a warm rug. In the complete exhaustion which follows its flight for life, it is particularly necessary to guard it from the dangerous effects of a change of temperature. But another precaution has to be taken, much more remarkable. When the eland is comfortably wrapt up in the rug it receives a subcutaneous injection of some liquid the constitution of which my travellers have unfortunately not been able to discover. Probably it is morphia or something of the sort, for a few minutes after the injection a stupefied condition supervenes and the antelope quickly falls into a deep sleep. Without this injection the creature would scarcely live a quarter of an hour ; before this method of treating them was hit upon, they used to die from heart strain. When it has gone to sleep, it is carried back to the camp and laid in a secluded place, where it remains in a deep sleep for nearly twenty-four hours. On its awakening it is led to a milch-cow which has been previously secured, and it is trained to regard the cow as its foster-mother. The cow's legs have first to be tied, for she soon realises that it is not her own calf but a new arrival from the veldt. After a few days the foster-parent and child come to know each other.   In the present instance a delay of some months was necessary before my traveller considered the young ante_lopes strong enough to undergo the arduous journey to the coast.   Johannsen occupied himself in the meanwhile in carry_ing out hunting expeditions in all directions and thus securing some valuable additions to my collection.   In the accompany_ing photograph the elands may be seen on their way down

Transport from the interior of Africa with eland antelopes.

to the coast harnessed to a buggy with a team of oxen, mules, and zebras.

I may suitably terminate this chapter by stating my opinion that science is in all probability still incompletely acquainted even with the larger members of the world's fauna.   My travellers explore the most remote parts of every continent, and it is therefore natural that they should often bring back information which is of great interest to zoologists. They often hear stories from the natives concerning strange animals which, from the descriptions given, would appear to be unknown to Europeans.   It might be supposed that these are mere cock-and-bull stories, either exaggerated descriptions

of well-known animals, or else intentional fabrications.   But
such is not usually the case.   Much more often, the information given by the natives will lead to the discovery of new
species, if the instructions of the savages be properly carried
out.   For instance, the case of the discovery of the remains
of the giant sloth in South America is famous, and all my
readers will remember the excitement which was caused when
the existence of the okapi was made known.   Native reports
are more reliable than is commonly supposed.

Some years ago I received reports from two quite distinct
sources of the existence of an immense and wholly unknown
animal, said to inhabit the interior of Rhodesia.   Almost iden-
tical stories reached me, firstly, through one of my own
travellers, and, secondly, through an English gentleman, who
had been shooting big-game in Central Africa.   The reports
were thus quite independent of each other, and, as a matter
of fact, the Englishman and my traveller had made their way
into Rhodesia from opposite directions, the one from the north-
east and the other from the south-west.   The natives, it
seemed, had told both my informants that in the depth of the
great swamps there dwelt a huge monster, half elephant, half
dragon.   This, however, is not the only evidence for the existence of the animal.   It is now several decades ago since
Menges, who is of course perfectly reliable, heard a precisely
similar story from the negroes ; and, still more remarkable, on
the walls of certain caverns in Central Africa there are to be
found actual drawings of this strange creature.   From what
I have heard of the animal, it seems to me that it can only
be some kind of dinosaur, seemingly akin to the brontosaurus.
As the stories come from so many different sources, and all
tend to substantiate each other, I am almost convinced that
some such reptile must be still in existence.   At great expense, therefore, I sent out an expedition to find the monster,
but unfortunately they were compelled to return home without having proved anything, either one way or the other.   In
the part of Africa where the animal is said to exist, there are

enormous swamps, hundreds of square miles in extent, and my travellers were laid low with very severe attacks of fever. Moreover, that region is infested by bloodthirsty savages who repeatedly attacked the expedition and hindered its advance. Notwithstanding this failure, I have not relinquished the hope of being able to present science with indisputable evidence of the existence of the monster. And perhaps if I succeed in this enterprise naturalists all the world over will be roused to hunt vigorously for other unknown animals; for if this prodigious dinosaur, which is supposed to have been extinct for hundreds of thousands of years, be still in existence, what other wonders may not be brought to light?

# CHAPTER IV.

## CARNIVORES IN CAPTIVITY.

SEEING how intimately I have always been associated with wild animals, it is a remarkable circumstance that I should never have met with any severe accident. That I have escaped the jaws of the tiger, the crushing feet of the elephant, the horns of the buffalo, the cruel coils of the serpent, is no doubt partly due to the prudence and care which I always observe in dealing with these creatures; but I am bound to add that wild animals are not nearly so savage as is commonly imagined. On the contrary they are often most affectionate, and I have had many friends among lions, tigers and panthers, which were no harder to handle than pet dogs. Moreover their affection is very enduring, and survives long after they have found another home.

The following is a remarkable instance of the memory of carnivores for people who have won their confidence. Forty years ago or more I bought a pair of young tigers, one of which caught a bad cold, which produced in him an affection of the eyes from which he became blind. For months I nursed him with the utmost care, going every day to his cage to make him as comfortable as possible, so that a very intimate relationship between us grew up. At length my devotion was rewarded and he completely recovered. Later on, he and his mate were sold to Professor Peters of the Berlin Zoological Gardens, and here the pair lived for many years; but to the day of his death the tiger whom I cured retained a most faithful attachment to me. Often I did not see him for long periods together, but, notwithstanding this, he would

always fall into the most violent excitement on hearing my voice in the distance ; and when I came up he would purr like a cat, and was never satisfied till I had gone into the cage and spent some little time with him. Often on these occasions have the public stood round in astonishment at the spectacle of this strange meeting. In memory of this tiger I had a water-colour painted for me by the animal painter Leutemann, which is still in my possession.

My animal friends are scattered about in many parts of the world, carefully guarded behind bolts and bars. Their life is not so long as ours ; old age and death come very quickly upon them ; and hence most of my friendships are things of the past. One of my oldest friends is a lion now resident in the Zoological Gardens at Cologne. This lion came from North Africa, and was one of a pair purchased by me when five years old from a Belgium menagerie in 1890. They were exceedingly handsome and perfectly tame, so that, although I only had them for two months, that period was sufficient for a lifelong friendship to grow up. I spent a considerable time with the animals every day and was very sorry when at last they had to go. One went to the Zoological Gardens at Hamburg and the other to Cologne. The one that stayed in Hamburg died several years ago, but the other is still alive, and, though now old and infirm, he still remembers me. Once when I was travelling in a train to Cologne I made a bet that he would recognise me without seeing me, if I merely shouted to him from some distance off. And I proved to be right ; for as soon as he heard the sound of my voice, the old lion came up to the bars and would not rest until I had greeted and stroked him.

I once made a similar experiment in the Zoological Gardens at Bronx Park in New York. There lived there two lions and a tiger with whom I had once been well acquainted but whom I had not seen for a long time past. The director, Dr. Hornaday, did not believe that the animals would recognise me ; but he was wrong. No sooner had I entered the door and

approached the den, than the creatures became attentive and
stared at me like a human being who saw a familiar face but
could not put a name to it. But the moment that I called out
the names by which I used to address them in Hamburg
they sprang up and ran to the bars, purring loudly while I
stroked and caressed them. There could scarcely be more
convincing evidence of the excellent memories which carnivores possess or of the fidelity which they show to
friends.

It is not necessary to go as far as New York to find evidence of this fidelity, as it can be seen any day in my animal
park at Stellingen. Here any sceptic may convince himself
that the wild beasts know and love their master. They
crouch down by the bars, lick my hands, and are delighted
when I stroke them. I am fond of all animals, but carnivores
are my special favourites. So attached to them do I become
that, in spite of their costly upkeep, I often keep them with me
for a longer time than is desirable from the strictly business
point of view.

In the open carnivore gorge at Stellingen there is on
view an old lion who has been in my possession for eighteen
years. His name of "Trieste" was given him many years
ago when he was imported through the port of that name.
Trieste is a great Somali lion, very handsome when he was
young, and even now thoroughly majestic in his carriage.
Being by trade a performer, he has covered in his professional travels a considerable portion of the earth's surface.
The exhibition at Chicago in 1893 and that at St. Louis
in 1904 were both honoured by the presence of Trieste as a
guest. Now that his life's work is over, he is in much better
circumstances than many human performers who have grown
old in their profession. And Trieste is worthy of his good
fortune. He is as tame, true and faithful as a dog; indeed
I often treat him as if he were a dog. One day last summer
I noticed with sorrow that my old friend was lame, and upon
further observation I found that he was suffering pain.

After a close examination I found that on each of the animal's hind feet two claws had grown into the flesh. Now it may well be supposed that the necessary operation would be a matter of great difficulty—the animal firmly bound and the operators going in danger of their lives. But nothing can be farther from the truth. In such matters Trieste can be treated as though he were a sensible human being. Having been ordered to lie down, his claws were clipped with large sharp clippers, and the points were drawn out. During

Having a bath.

the whole procedure, which was by no means painless, the lion kept perfectly still. For several days the wounds were well washed out ; they soon healed, and he is now once again well and happy.

As a corresponding instance of tameness among tigers, I may mention a great Siberian tiger, which in the summer of 1893 was sold from Vladivostock to the Zoological Gardens in Hamburg, and thence came into my possession. This animal was really as tame as any household pet. I could do anything with him, and used even to take him with me into my sitting-room. He was, moreover. a beautiful creature, and as I was very loth to part with him, he remained over a year in my care. As I ascertained later, the animal had been brought up quite young at Vladivostock, and I have it on certain authority that he ran about free for more than a year, without ever causing any mischief. Every morning, when I went my rounds, I visited my favourite and caressed him. If I happened to pass his cage in haste without noticing him, he would attract my attention with a mewing sound, to remind me that I had not spoken to him.

I fear that much of what I now write will be received by many with incredulity, for in the popular estimation carnivores conjure up a vision of all that is faithless, savage, and cruel. But it is certainly a mistake to call them cruel. It is, their nature in the wild state to hunt living prey, and they have to kill in order to live. We are too prone to forget how many millions of animals are hunted and slaughtered, both by land and sea, to provide food for human beings ; and it is as reasonable to accuse mankind of cruelty on this score, as it is to accuse carnivores. Carnivores love their young just as we do, and can also be affectionate and faithful. Of course one often comes across black sheep, but that is due either to their having been caught when adult, or to their being the victims of bad rearing.

All carnivores without exception, when they are caught young and are properly treated, are capable of being brought up as domestic pets. Their so-called wild nature does not break out unless something happens to put the animals in a rage ; and this, after all, is just the same with domestic animals. As to what can be achieved in the way of taming wild animals, I have certainly had more experience than any other human being. Both intelligence and love of animals are essential to success in taming. Then it is quickly discovered that among animals, as among men, good and bad are mixed, and that, while the good will develop of itself, the bad can be suppressed. I shall shortly give some evidence, too, of the intensity of feeling which prevails among wild animals.

The management of carnivores which have been captured in the adult condition is, of course, very difficult, and it is quite impossible to train such animals to the extent that is now considered quite ordinary in the case of young animals. To deny this is simply nonsense. Nothing more than a superficial polish can be imparted to animals which are grown up when caught.

About fifteen years ago I obtained from Calcutta the most savage, as also the largest and heaviest, Bengal tiger that I have ever come across. I received him from the Zoological Gardens in Calcutta, only a few months after he had been captured. During his first few days in Hamburg he was in a furious rage; whenever I approached his cage he would fly to the bars and stretch his paws through in his savage attempts to seize me. I naturally did not relish this sort of thing, and kept at a respectful distance. However, I paid the animal a visit every day and showed him that his efforts to harm me were quite fruitless; as soon as I approached him I made a purring noise, addressing him, as it were, in his own language. As time wore on the animal became quieter. To be sure, as soon as I appeared he still sprang angrily against the bars of his cage, but he no longer struck at me with his paws. After a week I began to take him a piece of meat every day, for the way to the heart lies through the stomach —a proverb which applies not only among the lower animals. After four weeks I could just venture to touch the great beast; I had to keep my eyes open, however, for now and again during these experiments he would lash out at me with his claws. I kept this tiger for about three months, by the end of which time he had realised that nobody wished to hurt him. When he saw me he would come quietly to the bars and allow me to stroke him. I had succeeded in curing him of his ferocity, and moreover, after he left me, he does not seem to have relapsed, for in the Dresden Zoological Gardens

—whither he went—he allowed both the director of the Gardens and his own attendant to stroke him.

I remember, however, an even more remarkable case. In the summer of 1905 my brother, John Hagenbeck of Colombo, sent me a panther which had been in captivity only a short time. I gave this panther to the Swiss sculptor, Urs Eggenschwyler, who designed the beautiful rocky cliffs in the Stellingen Gardens. Eggenschwyler, who is unusually fond of animals, and who keeps for his pleasure a number of lions and panthers, was delighted with my present, and commenced at once to train the animal. In less than a fortnight, he had so far succeeded that it would turn round and round in its cage when he commanded it to do so. The artist had previously taught this trick in Zurich to a number of other animals which had been captured adult, and on the present occasion he was so successful that in less than four weeks the panther could be made to revolve as many as eight times in succession. The animal's obedience was, of course, rewarded with a piece of meat.

Perhaps after what I have said my readers may think that after all there is nothing very alarming about the great carnivores—that they are, in fact, not much more than a kind of meat-eating lamb. In my chapter on the training of wild animals I shall show that the training is by no means so simple as it sounds. Of its danger there can be no question, but nevertheless it is the case that many of those who deal with the carnivores professionally owe their lives to the good temper of the animals.

In this connection I remember an extraordinary nocturnal adventure, which would, I imagine, have alarmed the bravest of us. In the beginning of the sixties I was bringing from Cologne to Hamburg a huge collection of animals, which I had obtained in France and Belgium. Among the animals there was a four-year-old lion, which I had obtained from the Zoological Gardens in Cologne, then quite recently established. The lion was placed in a great kennel and, along with all the

S ellingen babies.

other animals, was installed in the railway van. A man named Druard, who was inspector of the Zoological Gardens, and had previously held the position of head-keeper in Christian Berg's menagerie, was in charge of the animals during the journey. Everything having been satisfactorily arranged, Druard closed the door of the van, and made himself thoroughly comfortable.

The train rumbled on through the night and the unsuspecting keeper dosed peacefully, perchance enjoying some sweet dream. Suddenly, in the midst of his slumbers, he felt a great weight upon his chest, and awoke with a start. In the darkness, not a yard from him, there shone two greenish lights, and he felt hot fetid breath on his face. Overcome with terror he peered into the gloom and could just discern the shaggy outline of a lion's mane. For a second he lay quite still, hoping that it was only a nightmare—vain hope, however ; the lion had escaped from his cage, and was amusing himself by paying a visit to the solitary sleeper. Druard was accustomed to dealing with animals, and he knew that this lion was a good-tempered one. So he decided at once that the best thing to do was somehow or other to tie the animal up. For the rest, he must share the place with the lion until the next station, and make the best of his awkward situation. Luckily no trouble broke out between the lion and the other animals. Had it done so, the man would never have lived to tell the tale. Druard quietly untied a sash which he wore round his body, and placed it like a cord round the lion's neck. Then, groping his way through the dark and jolting van, he succeeded in fastening the other end of the sash to the handle of the door. At the next station he sounded the alarm, lights were brought, and the lion was led back to his cage—a stronger box being provided for him before the journey was continued. Thus ended a bloodless adventure, which nearly cost a careless man his life.

The occasions on which human beings are attacked by captive carnivores are fortunately rare. But quarrels be-

tween the beasts themselves are more frequent, unless they
are carefully watched and separated from each other when
necessary.    And among the lower animals, as with ourselves,
the trouble usually arises over the gentler sex.    In a troupe
which Heinrich Mehrmann exhibited in Chicago, Berlin, and
elsewhere, there was a fine lion called " Leo" and a great
Bengal tiger called "Castor".    The lion was a bachelor,
while the tiger was mated to a beautiful Bengal tigress.    As ill-
luck would have it, when the breeding time arrived the tigress
proved an irresistible attraction to the lion.    The tiger, naturally irritable, and perhaps not unreasonably jealous, regarded
the lion's proceedings with disapproval, and the relations between the two rivals became strained.    The tiger was as
jealous as a Turk ; the lion as determined as the consciousness
of his own strength could make him ; the tigress was prepared
impartially to receive the attentions of either.    One morning,
as I was walking in my Zoological Garden at Neuer Pferdemarkt, I heard a terrific roaring which proceeded from the
direction of the great open-air cage.    I immediately hurried
to the spot.    Sure enough, a bloody duel was taking place
between the lion and the tiger.    Both were standing on their
hindlegs and were giving each other such mighty boxes on
the ears that their hair was already scattered about.    The
sight of the two great animals standing in battle array, and on
the point of rushing into a life-and-death struggle, I shall never
forget.    They were, however, much too valuable for this love
intrigue to be allowed to end with the death of either of them.
The keeper of this division, who happened to be near, sprang
into the little front cage and from thence into the big cage
where the animals were, and succeeded in separating the combatants by shouting and cracking his whip.    Many tufts of
hair and pools of blood were left to show where the fight had
been.

All carnivores, but especially lions and tigers, are extremely ill-tempered at breeding times.    In trained troupes,
where both lions and lionesses are necessary, it is frequently

essential to remove the males from the troupe altogether during certain periods.   Where the trainer omits to do this, he
runs great risk of trouble, and he himself may be mauled.
Even with my best four-footed friends, I have found that
during these periods they are apt to be surly and quite intractable.   The ardour of these animals is boiling hot, and
their jealousy of any possible rival is even greater than their
tenderness towards the object of their affection.   It is very
remarkable, too, that a love-sick lion is not only jealous of his
own kind, but also of any human being—the keeper not ex-
cepted—who may happen to approach his cage.

It is my experience that lions, if they are well taken care
of, will frequently live for more than thirty years.   It happens
sometimes that animals come into my possession, which I
have previously known well, perhaps years before.   For instance, in a menagerie which I purchased a few years ago
there was a lioness that I had already possessed twenty
years earlier.   It was of course difficult to find a purchaser
for her.   At that time I had just supplied a lioness for breeding purposes to the Zoological Gardens at Cologne, but
Director Funk, who at that time had the management of the
institution, was not quite satisfied with the specimen.   I
therefore invited him to come to Hamburg to choose another,
and in this way it came about that the old lioness was paid
a great compliment.   She was very well preserved, was of
unusual beauty, and still possessed her full set of teeth.
Moreover, when I came up to her cage, accompanied by Mr.
Funk, she sprang to and fro vigorously in her delight at seeing me.   Thus it happened that of all the lionesses, Mr.
Funk decided to choose this one.   When I told him the
true state of affairs—which was, perhaps, ungallant to the
old lioness, but was honourable to the would-be purchaser—
he refused to believe me, and supposed that I was unwilling
to sell such a beautiful specimen.   If I had allowed him to
take her, however, he would not have derived much satisfaction from this brood-lioness, for according to my experience

in the matter these animals are thoroughly fertile up to the age of sixteen, but not after that time. The director, whose error was very naturally caused by the youthful appearance of the lioness, eventually took another specimen which has proved highly satisfactory.

Lions may be considered sexually mature at the age of two and a half years, but to obtain really strong offspring, it is desirable to wait for another year. In the case of tigers, according to my observations, sexual maturity arrives in captivity a year later than with lions. The capacity to reproduce their kind endures with all the cat-tribe for about twelve years, and expires therefore during the sixteenth or seventeenth year.

I had an experience in the breeding of jaguars about the year 1870, when a Hungarian traveller brought from Paraguay two pairs of large, full-grown jaguars. The jaguars, which the Hungarian had captured himself, were already well on in years. I should have much liked to possess these animals, but I was compelled to refrain from the purchase, as the price asked was too high for me ; they were bought by the menagerie owner, Manders, who in those days had the largest menagerie in England, and he succeeded in obtaining several litters from the two pairs, the young cubs being excellently brought up by their mothers.

Among many fortunate experiments, I succeeded in breeding two beautiful little cubs from a pair of captured ounces during the year 1906. The parents were cripples, each of them lacking a hind foot, and it was in consequence difficult to find a purchaser for them. I therefore arranged a nice secret recess in their cage, and placed the cage so that the animals could not be disturbed. Barely two months later, signs of mutual affection between the two animals were to be observed, and in the middle of May my keeper informed me that a couple of young ones had been born. Naturally, after this occurrence great care was taken to avoid disturbing the ounces in any way ; they were fed and watered, and the cage was

Tiger cubs.

cleaned in the afternoons, but with this exception the animals were left absolutely in peace.   After four days I removed for a moment the lid, which closed the secret recess, and I then saw the two pretty little cubs lying in a nest which the parents had lined with hair from their winter fur.   Four weeks later the father of this litter was found dead in his cage, but the mother and young are still living.

The lions and tigers in my animal-park are kept in the carnivore glen, which is not surrounded by a barrier, but is separated from the public by a deep trench only.   They are allowed out into the open air every day without exception dur_ ing both summer and winter.   The weather troubles them very little, and they range about in the open much more during the winter than they do during the summer when it is hot. Every morning the sliding door between the cage and the glen is opened, so that the animals can go out ; they can, however, always return to the inner den if they please. Nature comes to the help of the animals and makes it possible for them to adapt themselves to the climate.   We have ob- served that the exotic animals, which are not confined in winter, grow a thick fur that protects them from the cold.   I am quite convinced that it is possible to transplant lions to any climate whatever, provided they are allowed out into the open during spring when they are young.   I take it, that such lions would eventually grow in winter a woolly covering beneath their hair, exactly as is found to be the case with Siberian tigers and panthers.

Interbreeding occurs between lions, tigers, and other kinds of cats, even without the intervention of man, and it is therefore not very difficult to carry out experiments in cross- breeding.   I have bred many young from lions and tigers ; of such hybrids, I possess at the present time a male five and a half years old, and another male and a female of three and a half.   The father was a small Somali lion and the mother a small tigress, the offspring of the cross being, curiously enough, considerably larger than their parents.   The one male hybrid weighs as much alone as the two parents together.    They are powerful animals with strong heads, and are faintly striped. When people see them for the first time they wonder whether they are looking at lions or tigers.    These queer creatures are unusually tame, and of a very mild disposition.    According to our experiments thus far, they have unfortunately never been found to be fertile.

The youngest of the Hagenbeck family.

A cross between a panther and a puma was undertaken at my suggestion in a certain small English menagerie.    A number of young ones were born, but they all died except one, and there was nothing very noteworthy about the survivor.    I have also heard of a cross between a tiger and a female panther, but the young one was born prematurely and had no vitality.    I know of another similar case. In a small German menagerie there was quite a happy marriage between a lion and a female panther.    The panther gave birth three times, but unfortunately she proved herself a monster wholly lacking in maternal feelings, for she proceeded to devour her own cubs. On one occasion the owner of the menagerie succeeded in taking away the young from their mother, but they did not live long, and he foolishly threw them away instead of preserving them in spirit for scientific purposes.

In the Zoological Gardens at Stuttgart, which are now unfortunately closed, some very interesting hybrids were bred by Herr Nill. These were a cross between the brown bear and the polar bear. A short time ago I saw some more of these animals, which are in the Zoological Gardens in London. They are large heavy creatures, but not larger than their parents. One of them is a very curious fellow, a piebald, his fur being half greyish-brown and half white.

The real difficulty in the treatment of captive carnivores begins, as we shall see in the next chapter, when one attempts to train them to perform; for here one is endeavouring to make the animals do what is contrary to all their natural instincts. All the difficulties, however, can be overcome by patience, by a careful study of the brute mind, and by a recognition of the good qualities which are to be found in every creature.

# CHAPTER V

## TRAINING WILD ANIMALS.

THERE is probably no sphere in which the growth of humanitarian sentiment has been more striking than in the treatment and training of performing animals. Obedience which in former days was due to fear is now willingly paid by the animal from motives of affection. The period when unfortunate animals were driven to jump over a bar from dread of a whip or a red-hot iron—a disgrace to the humanity of man!—is gone by. Sympathy with the animal, patience with its deficiencies, has brought about a perfection of education which cruelty altogether failed to secure. And at the same time relations between trainer and beast have improved too. The trainer is no longer a taskmaster, or the beast a slave. There subsists between them the wholesome and happy relation of teacher and pupil. The old crude method of training—if these stupid barbarities deserved to be called training ; torturing would have been a more appropriate expression—consisted in terrifying the animals with whips and red-hot irons, so that at the very sight of these implements they would fly through the cage, and in doing so would leap over whatever obstacle was placed in their path.

Many years ago I saw at an auction in England four "trained" lions, whose whiskers had been scorched off and who were frightfully burned about their mouths. Naturally, when the animals were treated in this way, it was no uncommon thing for the trainers to be attacked and torn to pieces ; nor can one blame the lions and tigers which at last turned round upon their tormentors, for their better natures

Indian juggler with dancing bear.

had been completely destroyed. Their lives were rendered insupportable, and they acted only in self-defence.

It is a complete mistake to suppose that carnivores are vicious by nature; they are susceptible to kindness and good treatment, and will repay trust with trust.

In my younger days I had plenty of opportunities of ob-serving these barbarous shows, not only in Germany but also in England; and from the beginning I felt a desire to institute a more rational and humane method of training. Performances with carnivores were first shown in Hamburg many years ago by the trainer Batty. This daring man—for the trainer of those days certainly carried on his profession in the face of very real danger—worked, if I remember rightly, with six lions. The exhibition consisted in terrifying the animals, and then driving them around the cage so that they were com-pelled from sheer fright to leap over barriers that were pushed in from the outside. Finally Batty would stand near the exit, fire several shots from a carbine, and then retire from the scene. The surprising part of such a performance was that the animals did not attack the trainer.

There were, of course, individuals among the trainers who treated their animals as well as was possible under the brute-force system then prevailing. One of these was a man named Cooper. Cooper worked with a large troupe of lions, and with such success, that the American circus-owner Myers took over both the trainer and the lion troupe, into the tent-circus, with which he made a tour through Germany and Austria-Hungary. Cooper, an intelligent and experienced man, was well aware of the fact that for the successful train-ing of performing animals it is essential to discard at an early stage from the troupe any animal which evinced lack of intel-ligence, or ill-temper—a necessary step if an element of danger and uncertainty is not to attach itself to the exhibition.

Whilst he was working with Myers, this animal-trainer had a serious adventure with some lions which he had procured from me. I received one day from Myers, an

inquiry whether I could supply him with some lions. It
happened that I had just purchased a whole collection of
animals, among which were some lions that had always been
used for performing purposes. Cooper came himself to
Hamburg, inspected the animals, and, having completed the
purchase, took them with him immediately to Brussels. At
Brussels he made the grave mistake of putting all the lions,
old and new, together, instead of slowly and gradually allowing the animals to become acquainted with each other. The
new lions had never worked with other specimens and were
strange to their surroundings. They became irritable and
nervous, and when Cooper tried to drive them with a whip
to the performance of the tricks, a catastrophe occurred. One
of the new lions, and that the best-tempered of them, fell upon
Cooper and mauled him savagely. Thus by a mutual misunderstanding, a humane trainer was wounded by a perfectly
good-tempered lion, and the unfortunate man had to spend
some time in bed before his wounds were healed.

This event gave rise to a somewhat ludicrous incident.
On the day after the accident I received a telegram from
Myers from Brussels, saying that he wished me to take back
one of my lions, as it was ill. When the telegram arrived,
although I still knew nothing about the accident, I did not
take the statement very seriously. I knew that the lion had
been in perfect health at the time of delivery, so if anything
had gone wrong since it must be due to an accident. I wired,
therefore, my refusal to take back a lion which had been delivered in good health and for which I had received payment.
Next day another telegram arrived which ran as follows:
" Your lion is dead : what shall I do with him ? " To this I
promptly replied : " Pickle him if you like ".

A few weeks later, when I had nearly forgotten the whole
affair, a cask of pickled lion actually arrived in Hamburg for
me ! Probably the stupid fellow thought that by carrying out
the advice tendered to him in my ironical answer, he would be
putting himself in the right. Of course I immediately returned

the official invoice to the station and refused to take delivery of the cask. Myers next tried to bring an action against me, but here too he failed, for when the lion's remains were examined it was proved that he died from ill usage. The skin around the vital parts was covered with extravasated blood, and all over the body there were marks of the terrible blows which the animal had received at the hands of the people who had rescued Cooper at the time of the accident.

The treatment which the animals received from the old German animal trainers—such as Kreutzberg, Martin, Kallenberg, Preuscher, Schmidt, Dagersell, and Kaufmann, all of whom travelled mainly in Germany and Austria—was on the whole less cruel than that I have just been describing, for they used to exhibit only such animals as had been tamed from their earliest days and which were therefore much less difficult to train. Some of these men used to give quite interesting performances, although, as they exhibited in small waggon-cages (contrasts indeed to the great arenas which are now used) it was not really possible for them to accomplish much.

A son of the old Kreutzberg introduced a new branch of animal performance, which in barbarity it would be difficult to surpass. When Karl Kreutzberg was travelling through Spain with a troupe of seven lions, obtained from me, the people wished him to show them a fight between a lion and a bull. Kreutzberg was an enterprising fellow. He foresaw the popularity of the proposed exhibition, and, immediately falling in with the idea, set to work in an ingenious manner to make the performance, brutal as it was, a success. Kreutzberg had hitherto been giving his performances in the oval waggon-cages, which were then general, and are still sometimes to be seen. For the lion and bull fight, however, he had an especially large cage constructed, and devised a clever plan for bringing the two beasts into collision. The bull was led round and round the lion's cage. The lion, maddened with hunger—he had received no food—made furious attempts to seize his prey.    Then the performance itself commenced ; the bull was first led into the big cage, and then, after a pause—during which the excitement of the audience reached fever-heat—the lion was let loose.    With a roar the great cat hurled himself upon the bull and dragged it to the ground ; for as a rule the bull makes but a poor defence.    The Spaniards and the Portuguese were delighted with this bloody scene, the fame of which spread far and wide. Kreutzberg made a great deal of money out of the show.

Other animal trainers have attempted, both in Spain and in the south of France, to imitate this performance of Kreutzberg's, but without success.    They did not go to work with the same ingenuity as Kreutzberg.    Instead of exhibiting the fight in a cage, they usually employed a large arena for the purpose.    Now when a lion or tiger is let out of his small cage into a large arena, he becomes nervous and embarrassed, and in his bewilderment quite forgets his hunger.    On three occasions I have supplied lions for these fights.    In two cases the lion paid no attention to the bull, and the bull took no notice of the lion ; neither wished to come to closer quarters with the other.    On the third occasion, however, the upshot of the performance was more exciting.    The bull charged the lion and wounded him so severely that the king of beasts, after lingering miserably for several weeks, passed away to the shadowy hunting grounds of his fathers.

But these barbarous methods of training animals are now no longer in vogue ; they have become obsolete for this reason if for no other : that it is impossible to achieve by ill-treatment one-hundredth part of what can be done by humane and intelligent methods.    With the lower animals, as with human beings, real insight into their character can only be obtained by treating them sympathetically.    This essential fact, which is now understood by all successful animal trainers, ought in no way to surprise us, for the brute intelligence differs from the human in degree only, not in kind.    Animals soon perceive whether they are being treated sympathetically or otherwise, and quickly attach themselves to those who use them with kindness and consideration. Their memories, too, are usually very retentive, a fact highly important to the trainer's art. I have already explained to the reader in my chapter on carnivores in captivity that these animals are not so dangerous as people who know nothing about them suppose; indeed the majority of them, as I have already said, are by nature of a peaceful and even affectionate disposition. Strange as this may seem, it is nevertheless true.

It is now universally recognised that each animal has its own peculiar characteristics, its own idiosyncrasies over and above the general psychological character which it shares with all other members of its species. This is a discovery I had to make for myself, and a most important one it is for the trainer, for, I say without fear of contradiction, that no trainer is fit for his vocation who is unable to read the character of the individual animals which he has to train. And so it came about that when I introduced the humane system of training, as I may call it, I not only substituted for the whip and the red-hot iron a kindly method of educating the creatures (based upon an intelligent system of rewards and punishments) but I also instituted the practice of studying the character of each individual animal before including it in a troupe. At the present day all trainers worthy of the name follow this course. From the first moment that the animals come into possession of their teachers, they are carefully observed and have all their peculiarities noted with the view of applying to each the treatment best adapted to its temperament. Some animals require more encouragement than others; many, on the contrary, have to be treated sternly owing to their obstinate dispositions. Such differences as these must be known and acted upon by the trainer. It must be remembered that the trainer's task is beset with difficulties, for he is demanding from his pupils something which is altogether foreign to their nature. It is not natural for a lion

roaming the primeval forests of Africa to ride like a man on
the back of a horse, or for a tiger prowling through an Indian
jungle to amuse itself by jumping through a hoop.  Moreover,
not every lion or tiger can learn to perform tricks, however
much trouble may be taken with his tuition.  Some are hope-
lessly clumsy in their movements, many never learn the duty
of obedience, and others again are nervous and forget from
day to day what they are taught.

As I have already observed, it is a cardinal principle of
the new school to expel from the troupe any animals which
do not possess sufficient intelligence, or are too clumsy, to
become successful performers.  To recruit beasts indiscrimin-
ately is to court failure.  Each beast must be carefully
selected in accordance with its aptitude for the work it is
wanted to perform ; otherwise the success of an entire troupe
may be marred by the misbehaviour of a single ill-chosen
animal.  It is absolutely essential to discard at once any
animals which are unadapted to the work.  I have previously
related that on the occasion of my first attempt to introduce
the humane system of training, out of twenty-one lions only
four proved to be of any use for my purpose.  Nor is the
selection of the most likely performers always a very easy
matter.  There are animals which behave quite well at first,
and only show a dislike for the work later, when they are set
to perform with a large number of comrades ; at such times
they are apt to become very dangerous to the trainer if he
fails to notice the change which has come over them.

Let us consider the first stages in the training of a troupe
of performing animals.  We see lions, tigers, panthers, polar
bears, and dogs, all young and unsophisticated, which have
been selected because of their beauty, and because they
appear to possess characters which will fit them to become
performers.  The first thing is to accustom the creatures to
one another, for it would of course be very dangerous, and
probably disastrous, to let the whole medley of animals into
a common cage without preparing them in any way for meet-

Steady, boy, s eac

ing each other. The cubs are therefore lodged in a row of single cages which are separated from each other by bars only ; the young animals can all see each other and converse together in their own language. The teacher gives individual attention to each of his pupils, visiting and petting each one in turn so that they all come to know and love their master. After a considerable time the animals are brought out for their first joint lesson, which takes place in a large arena, under the superintendence of the trainer to whom they have been accustomed. As in a kindergarten school, there is no real work done in the first lesson ; the animals only learn to know one another more intimately, play about with each other and with their master, and make themselves familiar with their new surroundings.

From the first moment that the creatures are let loose in the arena, the trainer keeps a watchful eye upon every member of the incipient troupe, and has frequently to interfere to prevent a quarrel. All young animals (and for the matter of that, all old animals too) are very fond of play, but they are exceedingly apt to lose their tempers during the game, and to misunderstand each other's actions. Here, perhaps, a polar bear lumbers towards a lion and playfully tugs the latter's mane ; but the king of beasts misses the point of the joke, and gives his Arctic comrade a heavy box on the ears. This might be the beginning of serious trouble, but the trainer is quickly on the spot, and by a kindly blow on the ribs intimates to the lion that civility is expected during lessons. Or, again, it occurs to a tiger, who is perhaps by nature somewhat of a hooligan, to deal a blow with his paw at a panther which is peacefully trotting by him ; the panther spits furiously and crouches to spring, but the trainer is again instantly on the spot, and soon separates the two combatants. Even during this first lesson it is possible for the trainer to get some idea of the character of his animals, to distinguish which of them are peaceable and which pugnacious, which are obedient and which obstinate and self-willed. In the second lesson all the

9

apparatus necessary for more advanced training is placed in
the arena, for of course the programme of the proposed performance is thoroughly worked out before any beginning is
made with the actual training of the animals. A number of
blocks are piled up in the form of a staircase; and there is
a barrel upon which a tiger has to learn to balance himself.
The trainer carries a whip, but far more important than this
is the leather pocket, attached to his belt, for it is here that
he keeps the little pieces of meat which are to reward the
young carnivores for their obedience. The animals are let
loose in the arena, and stare with astonishment at the imposing
erection which they see before them. They are not allowed
long, however, to satisfy their curiosity; the lesson is begun
forthwith, for the trainer knows well that it is only when they
really get to work that he can form a sound judgment upon
the characters and abilities of the various members of his
troupe.

On the top step of the pyramid of wooden blocks a lion
is to stand; on the second highest step two tigers, then two
panthers, and in front, upon two blocks, the polar bears are
to learn to sit, whilst the dogs are to be trained to jump over
the backs of the panthers. The work of making the animals
understand what is required of them needs infinite patience
they have to be taught to take their own places on the pyramid, and it is long indeed before they realise that they must
stay there quietly and not jump down before they receive the
order to do so. And no less patience is required in making
the tiger grasp the fact that he is intended to maintain his
grotesque position upon the rolling barrel, for the great beast,
naturally enough, does not readily comprehend the object of
this performance.

From the very commencement every step in the proceedings has to be carefully thought out and pre-arranged, and
their respective parts in the performance have to be so
thoroughly drilled into all the animals that they acquire an
absolutely inveterate habit of doing the right thing at the

Lion on his block.

9 *

right moment. Thus when the stage of rehearsals is over, and the performance is given before an audience, the programme is worked through almost mechanically. As soon as the animals which are to compose a troupe have been chosen, each one is given a name of its own by which it is always called, and as they hear their names shouted whenever anything is required of them, they soon grow accustomed to the sound. The first thing to be done is to give each animal a definite place of its own, and with this object in view small blocks are placed round the arena by the wall, and each fourfooted performer must be taught to sit upon his own special block, and, after each trick which he has performed or after each scene in which he has taken part, to trot back to this block as a matter of course. This is the first thing for the animals to learn. The trainer therefore walks up to a lion and holds a piece of meat in front of him, trying in this way to lead the brute to a block. Or perhaps he uses rougher methods, and pulls the creature along by its hair. When the spot is reached, the reward is not yet earned; the lion has to climb upon the block, and only when he has done this does he receive his prize. It never occurs to the lion, however, that he is supposed to remain upon the block; and having eaten the meat he immediately leaps off and proceeds to enjoy himself in the arena. The trainer must then lead him back to the block, and make him stand upon it once more. This has to be repeated over and over again until at last the lion begins to understand what his master wishes him to do. The same process has to be gone through with every member of the troupe. When in this way they have all been taught to take up their correct positions round the arena, they are then ready to learn the more advanced parts of the training.

After a considerable period has elapsed and all the movements have been repeated many times over with each animal, the troupe at last reaches the stage at which they answer to their names like pet dogs, and will stand or sit patiently upon their blocks around the arena until they are called by their master. This is of course the first and easiest stage of their education.; but even as early as this, many turn out to be unfit for the work through viciousness or other fault. Punishment in these cases would be of no use. It would only make the animals more stubborn than before ; and if they were kept in the troupe their fellow-pupils would soon be spoilt by the bad example. There is nothing for it but to replace them by more promising animals. The next thing to be done is to teach the tricks with which the public is to be astonished. The living pyramid has to be constructed over and over again. The tiger needs many lessons before he can stand upon his rolling barrel. The reader may easily perceive how great is the strain on the temper of the animal trainer, when he understands how many hundreds of times each small movement has to be gone through, and that the slightest loss of self-control on his part would ruin the whole of the proceedings. But while he is careful to keep his temper, he must at the same time maintain the strictest discipline. As he leads them upward step by step in their difficult task, he must imbue them with the feeling that disobedience is an impossibility. I need hardly say that the arduous labour involved in training wild animals can only be successfully carried out by one who is really fond of them. A genuine affection is needful for the establishment of mutual confidence between teacher and pupils. Courage too is most essential, for it must never be forgotten that however domesticated they may appear to be, they are yet at heart wild animals, and in all wild beasts there remains— deep down, perhaps, but there all the same—some remnant of their primitive ferocity. There is therefore always a chance of some savage outburst of temper, and the teacher has to watch with a never-tiring eye for the smallest indication of any change in behaviour of any of his fearsome pupils. And this liability to outbreaks of temper increases with advancing age.'

If the few cardinal principles which I have mentioned be carefully followed out, the danger ought to be very slight.

In looking on at a performing troupe the spectators often think that the animals are in a very dangerous temper, and are ready at the first opportunity to seize their master and tear him to pieces. But this appearance of ferocity is merely show, put on for the purpose of making the entertainment more piquant. The ominous snarling and savage growling do not really mean anger ; and that the trainer very well knows. How seldom accidents happen my own experience testifies. Enormous numbers of performing animals and very many performing troupes have at one time or another passed through my course of instruction, and gone forth into the world to earn their living. Of all these hundreds, or rather thousands, of animals, accidents have occurred in only two cases. In one, at least, of these cases, the fault must be ascribed rather to the man than to the animal. The accident happened at the Chicago Exhibition in 1893 when a foolish young Englishman managed to make his way from among the sight-seers into the carnivores' den without my knowledge and contrary to my strict orders. He paid for his folly by being severely mauled by a lion, but the trainer succeeded in extricating him in time to save his life.

The other accident was more directly traceable to carelessness on our part. It occurred during the Industrial Exhibition in Berlin in 1896, and the victim in this case was my brother-in-law Heinrich Mehrmann. He was exhibiting a large troupe of mixed carnivores, among which was a black bear which I knew to be dangerous and had specially warned him against. Nevertheless, he continued the performances with this animal, and received two severe wounds, which kept him in hospital for a month. I take some credit to myself for the fact that these two are the only accidents which have occurred under the immediate management of my firm. I account for it by the extreme care with which I eliminate from the troupe all animals that do not seem thoroughly reliable.

I think I ought to say something about my brother

Wilhelm Hagenbeck, who was one of the early pioneers of
modern methods and has by his long experience become a
past-master in the art of training wild beasts. Nearly all the
troupes which he now exhibits have been collected and broken
in by himself, though of late years he has received some assistance from his son. One of his most remarkable achievements was the training of a young lion to ride on the back of
a horse and in that position to perform a variety of equestrian
tricks.

Wilhelm Hagenbeck also was the first to introduce troupes
of polar bears into the circus. Before his time it was held
that polar bears were untrainable ; and to him belongs the

Polar bears in the arena.

credit of showing the error of this view. With great patience
and care their education is quite practicable, though at certain
periods of the year they become extraordinarily restless and
intractable. At this season it requires all the tact and ability
that the trainer possesses to keep the creatures under control.
The other species of bears—Russian, American and Indian—
all take kindly to performing exhibitions during the first few
years of their lives. But even they, when they have reached
the age of three or four, are apt to become peevish and dangerous. Bears, although some of the most amusing of all performers, are responsible for more accidents than any other animals.

In the same way that many of the performing troupes
throughout the world have been trained in my establishment,
so too their masters have in many cases received their early

Hagenbeck in the lions' den.

lessons in the very same place. There they have learnt to distinguish the peculiarities and characters of different animals. They have learnt also the great lessons of tact and patience, which are perhaps the most essential of all the traits which go to make up the animal trainer. I myself have advanced greatly in knowledge and skill since my début at Chicago. I make a rule of almost always going into the animals' cages to make myself acquainted with their peculiarities.

I well remember the astonishment on one occasion of a party of officers and ladies who had come one Sunday afternoon to visit my Zoological Garden. I took them to look at a dozen young lions which were shortly to be sent to the Chicago Exhibition, but which had not yet completed their training. As I stroked them through the bars, one of the officers laughingly remarked that that was all very well with bars in between, but would be a very different matter if I were inside the cage. I thereupon walked into the cage, to his great surprise, and was soon surrounded by them. As they were moulting at the time I got so covered with their hairs that I very soon looked like a lion myself. Without any whip or other protection I put them through the elementary tricks which they had already learnt. By the time I had come out, the incredulity of the party had vanished and I was bombarded with hundreds of questions as to how I taught them to be so tame.

My first experience as an animal trainer was in the seventies. About this time I had sold to the negro Delmonico three lion cubs and three tiger cubs, which he proceeded to train for three months in my establishment in a sort of waggon-cage. Just before he left he dared me to go into this cage and say good-bye to my animals. Although at that time I had nothing like the experience which I now have, I took him at his word. Going into the cage I succeeded in taking the animals through all the tricks which Delmonico taught them, to the very considerable discomfiture of that individual.

Hazardous experiments like this do not always end so well. Of this I have from time to time seen not a few instances, though I myself have survived whole and sound.

About the time of the incident with Delmonico which I have just related, I had offered a number of young bears, hyænas, and lions to a French animal trainer. These he had accepted on the condition that I first made the animals thoroughly accustomed to one another's society. It was in my efforts to carry out this provision that the trouble arose. The first thing to do was to place the animals in contiguous cages, separated from one another, not by a solid partition, but merely by bars through which they could see one another. When they had thus become accustomed to one another's proximity, I removed the bars between the bears and hyænas, and was glad to find that they took very kindly to one another. After a little time longer, I took the final step of removing the bars which separated the lions on the one hand from the bears and hyænas on the other hand. At first all was peace and happiness : but, alas! it was only the calm before the storm. To the present day I cannot, for the life of me, conceive what it was that suddenly brought about a violent misunderstanding. The bears trotted up to the lions, whether with the intention of provoking a quarrel or merely in playful greeting I cannot say. But if they intended it to be playful, the fun fell flat. The lions failed to perceive it in that light, and in a moment the whole collection, lions, bears and hyænas, degenerated into a savage throng of snarling beasts. My position now was anything but pleasant. I could not venture personally among the infuriated animals, as I should almost certainly have been severely injured ; so I made a hasty exit from the cage and with considerable difficulty we managed to separate the ill-tempered creatures before much harm was done.

My first troupe of heterogeneous animals was organised in the seventies. It consisted of two striped hyænas, two dogs, two brown bears and a young Indian sloth-bear. These

Trans                    olar hea

seven animals had been placed together at so early an age that they knew nothing of life apart from each other's society. By this early and intimate association, the animals which live in nature in the most extreme hostility may be bred up as bosom friends. The lion and the lamb lying down together is no mere fable, though it can only be achieved by long and careful training. In the wild state, the lion looks upon the ox as his normal food, and his whole nature has to be changed if he is to be taught to treat it as a friend. The peace-loving goat which feeds on vegetables has to be profoundly-altered in constitution before he can be persuaded to make friends with the blood-thirsty tiger, whose very odour is ordinarily sufficient to terrify him. The panther and the sheep may be brought up as playfellows, the one forgetting its savage instincts and the other its fears. It is entirely due to the humane system of training that this triumph is due. My first experiment in this line was made in the summer of 1889. I had then already succeeded in accustoming to one another two tigers, two lions, two black and two ordinary panthers, three Angora goats, two black-headed Somali sheep, an Indian dwarf zebu, a Shetland pony and two poodles. Of course, the training began when they were all quite young, mostly at about six or eight months. This troupe was almost ready to be exhibited, when a misfortune very nearly brought the whole work to nothing. The carnivores were attacked by the cholera epidemic, previously described, and most of them died. The few that I was able to send to the Chicago Exhibition were not sufficient for producing any of these greater effects.

I have, however, not lost sight of these experiments, and am confident that the most jarring elements of the animal kingdom may be united to a degree not yet dreamt of by the general public. I should not begin to boast before I have succeeded; but I may say that I hope very shortly to place before the public some exhibitions of this kind which will throw all previous ventures into the shade.

There is practically no animal which by the exercise of

patience and intelligence may not be tamed to some degree. Even alligators have been broken in and exhibited. Various kinds of seals have been used for performing with great success; and they are undoubtedly well adapted to the circus. Who has not marvelled at the way in which they can balance any kind of object on the tip of their snout, or toss up balls and catch them again with mathematical accuracy as they fall? A quarter of a century ago the American, Woodward, performed real wonders in the way of training seals. Just as in well-trained troupes a genuine friendship exists between the trainer and his animals, so it often happens that a close friendship grows up between the animals themselves. When this happens the trainer will do well to take full advantage of it by working the animals together. As long as these friendships are between animals of allied species they seem natural enough. I remember an instance of a crowned crane and an ostrich from West Africa which had become inseparable while still in the enclosure and before training began. On another occasion a similar friendship was formed between a crane and a goose. But when the animals are of totally different species the alliance between them is more remarkable. Thus I remember a case in which an elephant contracted a friendship with a pony. So indispensable to the great monster did the society of this pony become, that he became melancholy and refused his food when he was separated from his little comrade.

The first mixed troupe which my father established consisted of a great Bengal tiger, an Indian panther and a fox-terrier. These three creatures were knit together in a firm bond of friendship. The fox-terrier gnawed the same bone as the tiger, and the latter never thought of injuring his little friend. It is, as I have said, more impressive when the animals which work together are in their natural environment grim enemies. Nothing but the fundamental principle of kindness and studying the animals' habits can crown these efforts with success. Take, for instance, the case of a lion and a horse which are to be taught to perform together. First they are fastened up within sight but out of reach of each other. When they have become accustomed to each other's smell and appearance they can then by gradual means be brought to eat and sleep in each other's presence. In fact, they become so used to one another that neither notices the other's presence. When this stage has been reached the greatest obstacle has of course been surmounted.

A few years ago a man came to me and asked for employment as a seal trainer. I happened at the time to possess five fine young seals, and, having a lively recollection of Woodward's delightful performances, I engaged the man at a wage of 25s. per week with the promise that for each animal he succeeded in training he should receive a bonus of £5. My man soon showed that he knew what he was about. After four months the seals had become such adept performers that they beat the tambourine, twanged the guitar, fired off pistols, fetched articles that were thrown into the water and did various other tricks. My trainer received his bonus, and we sold the seals to Barnum for the large sum of £500.

Yet more clever and adroit than seals are the Californian sea-lions. This is the species which performs those wonderful tricks so common in the circus. The sea-lion is the most lively of all pinnipeds and quickly becomes accustomed to our climate. They have been bred in various Zoological Gardens, at Cologne, Paris, Amsterdam, and Antwerp. The American, Woodward, was the first to attempt the training of these animals, but later on he had rivals in two young Englishmen, Willie and Charlie Judge, who worked for several years in my Garden. These two brothers were the first to show what might really be done with sea-lions.

The largest sea-lion which I have ever seen was one that I received in the year 1880 from my old friend Barnum. Although this great animal weighed well over a quarter of a ton it was so tame that it used to follow my father like a dog, and he took a special pride in looking after it entirely by himself. An amusing incident once occurred when he was engaged in feeding this creature. It was one Sunday when several hundred spectators had come to watch the animals being fed. My father carried over his arm a basket in which were contained the fish which he threw as food to his pet. When the basket had been half emptied, my father, thinking that the sea-lion had had enough, turned round to walk away. But the sea-lion was of a very different opinion. No sooner had my father shown his intention of leaving, than the great beast glided up with lightning speed behind him, and with a sudden movement tore off all the clothes from his back. It then collared the basket and with great apparent good nature proceeded to devour the remainder of the fish. My father beat a hasty retirement into the nearest corner, where he stood in the only position that was decorous—namely with his back to the wall. I had to hurry to fetch some more clothes for my father ; and when he reappeared, arrayed in these, he was received with loud cheers by the public. This occurrence must not be attributed to any uncertainty of temper in the sea-lion, but to my father's error in taking into the enclosure more fish than he intended to give the animal. It felt that it was being unjustly treated, and adopted its own method of remedying its grievance. So far from showing ill temper, the incident shows intelligence in the animal—an intelligence which, whether they be lions or tigers, elephants or seals, is the most essential quality for a performing animal to possess.

# CHAPTER VI.

## THE GREAT HERBIVORES.

THERE is a widespread belief among the public that the elephant is one of the most intelligent of animals, and I certainly think that this opinion is well founded. Individual peculiarities are very noticeable in these animals : they are wonderfully quick of apprehension, have remarkably retentive memories, and in their likes, as in their aversions, they display great intensity and depth of feeling. The elephant is a much cleverer creature than the horse, and his power of differentiation is almost human.

On the emotional side too, the psychology of these gigantic quadrupeds is most interesting. Darwin was surprised to find that a bull elephant did not accept all the cows which were brought to him, but showed favour to some and rejected others. Now this is a subject which I have had frequent opportunities of studying, and I have found that these beasts "fall in love" in the true sense of the word ; that is, they conceive a truly monogamous affection for one particular cow, and are not merely actuated by a general predilection for the opposite sex. I remember a striking case in point. Some years ago I had in my Zoological Garden a young bull elephant that had just arrived at maturity. This animal became enamoured of a young cow, and, his affection being returned, it was an interesting and touching sight to see them tenderly caressing one another. I decided to test the genuineness of the bull's marital affection by the introduction of a third party—a somewhat cynical proceeding, perhaps, but it was all in the cause of science. One day, whilst the bull was enjoying a doze, his loved one was led away and another, somewhat older, but to all appearances thoroughly lovable, cow introduced in her stead. When the elephant awoke he immediately discovered his loss, and paying not the least attention to the blandishments of the new cow, he raged about the yard in a pitiful state of agitation until his sweet-heart was restored to him.

Elephants are in all ways models of domestic virtue, for the parents' devotion to their children is as great as their love for each other. I have frequently had opportunities of observing this, but to me it has always been even more interesting to see the kindness with which other elephants —not belonging to the family at all—treat the young calves. The patience of the old elephants is, too, very often severely tried, for the calves are astonishingly skittish for such heavily built little animals. They are up to all sorts of mischief, and are especially fond of running under the legs of their elders and nudging them from below. The calves used to have regular wrestling matches with my Indian elephant drivers, and when a man was knocked down by his opponent the little brute would trample upon him in the greatest delight.

A great number of elephants have passed through my hands, and in my long experience of the creatures I have naturally grown to know their racial character, as well as the peculiar traits of particular individuals. Indeed on more than one occasion an elephant has come uncomfortably near putting an end to my career. Clever animals are liable to moods, with which it is not always possible to reckon, and at certain seasons the bulls are not to be depended upon and become very dangerous. One of my worst accidents happened at the end of the sixties. About that time I purchased a menagerie in Trieste, which included among the other beasts a female elephant which stood about eight feet high. She seemed to be a thoroughly good-tempered animal, her only fault being that she occasionally had the sulks—a not

Cow-elephants with their young a  S ellingen.

uncommon characteristic in all feminine creatures. I soon made friends with the cow, who was given the name of Lissy, and I never passed her stall without giving her a handful of food. I was therefore justified in supposing that I had quite won her heart, and, as she never showed any signs of violence, it did not occur to me that I might be dealing here with a grossly deceitful creature. The elephant was being taught a trick, in which she had to lift her keeper high into the air with her trunk, and then slowly set him upon the ground again. The word of command which was given her when she had to perform this simple exhibition of her tameness was, "Lissy, apport!" One day about noon I found Lissy alone in her stable, the keeper being absent. There must have been a devil in me, for I felt a desire to be embraced and raised on high by the cow, after the manner of her affectionate treatment of her keeper. I therefore went up to the elephant, stroked and fed her, and taking hold of her trunk I called out the word of command, "Lissy, apport!" Then followed one of the most vilely treacherous acts of which I have ever heard. Lissy began to obey the order, but I soon felt that she was bent on mischief, for the embrace of her trunk was unpleasantly vigorous, and I soared high into the air. But I was not quietly deposited once more upon my feet. Instead of this, Lissy dashed me violently against the wooden barrier in front of her stall, and I went flying over into the menagerie. I lay almost senseless upon the ground until the old keeper, Philipp, appeared and helped me home. Fortunately neither my head nor my side had hit the barrier, and no bones were broken, but I was terribly bruised and for weeks I could only hobble about with great pain. Whether the elephant was secretly amused at my plight I cannot say, but I know that after this incident I entirely lost my love for her.

On another occasion I had an adventure which was, if possible, even more dangerous. At the time of which I speak I was busy sending off a large collection of animals to America, among which there was a male elephant that stood six feet at the shoulder and possessed tusks eighteen inches long. At that time the animals had to be shipped from Bremen, and so I went down to the railway station in Hamburg to see all the beasts properly entrained, leaving the keeper to bring along the elephant. Whilst I was in a van stowing away boxes, the elephant, which was very restive, was brought in and fastened up in a corner. The people who had brought him then departed, leaving me alone with the great quadruped and one other man, who was also at work in

Dwarf elephant from the Congo.

the van. Suspecting no danger I paid no attention to the animal, but went on with my work. Suddenly I received a terrific blow from behind and saw two tusks gleaming on either side of me. I realised in a flash that the elephant was trying to impale me against the wall. The tusks squeezed me on either side, and the brute was pressing me against the wall, but by vigorous wriggling I managed to slip down between the tusks and fall beneath the giant's body. There I lay groaning on the ground, but the other man, whose attention had by this time been attracted, rushed to the rescue and hauled me into safety. The pain in my back was terrible, but once more I had escaped without serious injury. Luckily for me the bull had made a bad shot; his tusks had gone through both coat and waistcoat on either side of my body; had they been a couple of inches either to the right or the left he would have pierced me through and through, and there would have been an end of Carl Hagenbeck.

On another occasion—it was in the eighties—one of my elephants proved so dangerous that I was reluctantly compelled to sign his death warrant. The beast in question was a large working elephant, a male standing about seven and a half feet high. He had more than once given proof of his vicious temper, and one day he brought the matter to a climax by attacking and nearly killing one of the keepers. The man was only saved by the promptitude and courage with which another keeper, who had the power of influencing and soothing the elephant, came to the rescue. The animal was out of the stables at the time of this occurrence, and naturally he had to be conducted back to his stall with the greatest caution. Rapes and bread were given him in the hope of appeasing his wrath, but some stout ropes were brought along too. One of these was fastened to a hindleg, and another to a foreleg. I then went ahead with the rope attached to the foreleg, and on reaching the stable I wound it round an iron post, so that, in the event of the brute breaking loose from his drivers, his range of action would at least be limited to the neighbourhood of the stable. At last the elephant reached his stall and the rope on the hindleg was quickly passed through a ring attached to the wall. At this moment the fury of the giant broke out afresh. By the side of him stood two other elephants, and being securely bound, both before and behind, he launched his mighty weight sideways against the nearer of these with such energy that this other elephant—who was as large as the great hooligan himself—fell flat upon her side, and nearly upset the further one as well. I had seen some proofs of elephant prowess before, but never anything quite equal to this.

One naturally dislikes putting an end to a valuable animal,

but in this case I saw it would not do to hesitate any longer. At any moment a fatal accident might occur ; there was no help for it, the monster must be executed.   It happened, however, that I had to depart for England on the next day, and it was therefore necessary to postpone the unpleasant ceremony until my return.   In England I met Mr. Rowland Ward, the naturalist·   I happened to tell him about the elephant,

which I proposed to have killed on my return, and to my surprise he made a most original proposal·   If the elephant were to be had cheap, he said he would willingly buy him from me, for he believed he could easily find a "sportsman" to whom it would be worth fifty pounds to be able to say that he had once shot an elephant! I naturally jumped at the idea of saving some of my loss, and through

12° below zero.

Rowland Ward it was soon arranged that a certain Mr. W. should come to Hamburg within a week for the purpose of shooting big game in my Zoological Garden.   Sure enough, the two gentlemen arrived in Hamburg provided with a whole arsenal of different sorts of rifles, and it was duly arranged that the elephant hunt should take place the next day at Neuer Pferdemarkt.   I made all the needful preparations, and took care to notify the police, who decided to send representatives to see that there was no danger to the public.   The hunt was to begin at ten o'clock, and in order to make the scene as dramatic as possible I had the bull driven out into the yard at the back of the elephant house, and there firmly tethered to a wall, so that he could not possibly break loose. The wall itself was overlaid with planks two and a half inches thick in order to prevent the bullets rebounding.

Ten o'clock struck, and all the preparations were complete. All was in readiness, but the hero of the story did not appear. What could have happened? We waited for an hour, and then, as the sportsman still did not arrive, I hastened into the town to remind him of his engagement. I found him and brought him back to the hunting-ground, and at twelve o'clock we gathered round to see the hunter slay his game. The gentleman had brought along his arsenal, but now that he was in sight of the victim his sporting ardour seemed to have unaccountably left him. He fingered his murderous weapons, but did not fire the fatal shot. Presently one of my travellers, who happened to be present, offered to fire the shot, but this the owner of the elephant refused to allow. After further delay, I at last proposed to the embarrassed hero that the animal should be hanged, and to this he gave his consent.

The condemned giant was therefore driven back into the stable, and a noose was placed round his neck. The rope was wound round a pulley, attached to a cross-beam under the roof, and six of my men played the part of executioners. "One, two, three" I called out, and at the third shout they all hauled on the end of the rope. The bull almost immediately lost the ground under his feet, his head fell sideways, and in less than a minute he was dead. We found afterwards that his neck had been broken. Thus ended one of the strangest tragi-comedies which I have ever seen.

Elephants in captivity do not always die such a painless death as that which I have just described. The fate of the first elephant which we ever possessed was far less happy. My father purchased this beast from an English animal dealer in 1860; the price was only £80, for the creature was afflicted with a serious lameness in his right hindleg. We hoped the brute would recover from this malady, but instead of getting better his lameness grew worse, and eventually he became so weak that he could only with the greatest difficulty stand up again in his stall after he had once lain

60° below zero.

down. At last he grew so bad that he lay for two whole days groaning in his stall, and my father seeing that nothing could be done for him, sold the unfortunate animal to the Hamburg Museum. The authorities of this institution took him over with the intention of killing him themselves. But this was not such an easy matter as they had supposed. They first attempted to put an end to the poor beast by injecting poison, but although the quantity used would have pretty well sufficed to finish off the entire population of Hamburg, the wretched elephant survived the ordeal. At last, in desperation at the pertinacity with which the animal clung to life, the people fastened him up by the trunk, and stuck him like a pig.

The reader may be inclined to infer from all these stories of accidents and other misfortunes that I have had ill-luck with elephants, and that they are very difficult creatures to manage in captivity. There is no doubt that they are apt to be awkward customers on occasion, and to the dangerous incidents which I have related I could add others of a similar character. Some of my elephants, for instance, once ran amok in Munich. Nevertheless, the vicious elephants are the exceptions. Most of my trunked friends live in my memory not because of their objectionable propensities but because of their intelligence, their good nature, and their wonderful fidelity. One of the most docile and affectionate beasts which I have ever known was a bull which I obtained some twenty years ago from a Hamburg trader. He stood seven feet high, and had tusks measuring two feet. When this animal was first offered to me he was still on the high seas, on the passage to Europe, but from the accounts of him which I received I gathered that he was unusually tame. As a rule, I am loath to buy male elephants, because, as I have previously explained, after they arrive at a certain age they are subject to periodic moods, during which their tempers are exceedingly uncertain. When the ship arrived in port I went on board to inspect the bull, and I speedily discovered that the stories I had heard of his tameness were in no way exaggerated. The poor beast was in a pitiful plight, however. It was already late in the autumn, and he was standing on the deck, in the open air, literally shaking and trembling with cold. Various other symptoms made it obvious that he was in ill-health. I thereupon agreed with the owner to take the animal to Neuer Pferdemarkt to see if a short residence there would improve his condition. A good warm stable, a nice straw bed, and careful nursing under my personal supervision, soon worked wonders, and in a week's time I was able to ratify my purchase.

The intelligence and affectionate disposition of this elephant were quite remarkable. After I had taken care of him for a few days he would call to me with trumpeting tones whenever he heard my voice or my step, and would beg for an extra morsel of food, with which I used always to indulge him. I baptised him "Bosco," and under this name he afterwards became famous in the circus world.

It was not long, only four weeks in fact, before a would be purchaser of Bosco appeared upon the scene in the shape of an American menagerie owner, who possessed a circus in Buenos Ayres. Before buying Bosco, however, the American desired that he should learn various tricks, and for this purpose it was arranged that the elephant should remain another six weeks in my possession. In the meanwhile I sold the American a troupe of performing lions, and these he sent off to Buenos Ayres, he himself remaining behind in order to take personal charge of Bosco on the passage across the Atlantic. I applied myself forthwith to the education of Bosco, and found him a marvellously apt pupil. All elephants are intelligent, but the quickness with which my present pupil understood what was required of him was simply astounding. The simple, old-fashioned tricks, such as used to be exhibited in all circuses, he learnt in a few days. He learnt in one day to lie down, and to sit down, at the word of command. In less than four weeks he would sit himself at a table, pull the bell, allow himself to be served by a monkey, drink out of a bottle, eat off a plate, and in short would dine in the most orthodox human fashion. He had in fact become an accomplished performer. After about six weeks my friend the American departed, highly delighted with Bosco. Over in South America he was very successful, constantly having a full house, and making large profits. Four months later he was once more in Europe, wishing to make further purchases, and I was again able to satisfy him in this direction.

My acquaintance with Bosco, however, was destined to be renewed, and that in an unexpected manner. One day, about two years later, I returned from a journey and was greeted with the joyful news that my favourite had returned from America, and was even now lodged in my own stables. It was already pretty late in the evening, but to me it was as though I was receiving a visit from an old friend, and, seizing some sandwiches as a welcome for my great pet, I hurried to the stables. In the menagerie it was nearly dark, and on reaching the door I shouted " Hallo, Bosco," and immediately a joyful cry rang out from the distance. As I came nearer Bosco began gurgling in his throat, after the manner of all his kind when anything pleases them very much. As soon as he could reach me he seized me by the arm, drew me close up to him, and licked me all over my face, all the time gurgling loudly. It was most touching to see the delight of the great quadruped at meeting his old master once more, and when it is remembered that the animal was only a few weeks in my possession—though, it is true, we were close friends during that time—this episode constitutes a convincing proof, I think, of the excellent memories possessed by these huge beings.

The rapidity with which elephants can be trained is very remarkable. Once, many years ago now, I was asked by the director of a theatre in Breslau to supply him with a young elephant which had been trained for riding. The animal was to take part in an exhibition, and was to be delivered in about a fortnight. Unfortunately I was just about to start upon a journey, which, of course, prevented me from beginning to train the young elephant; and as in those early days I was still proprietor, traveller, correspondent, and trainer all in one, the education of the beast could not be commenced until my return. I arrived home only two days before the expiry of my time limit. The first two hours of the training were exceedingly arduous, but after that time

I had obtained some control of my pupil. After four hours he had so far grasped what was required of him that he would lie down when commanded to do so, would allow me to clamber on to his back, and would, again at the word of command, stand up once more. That was the first day's lesson. On the second day I trained him to allow me to ride him to and fro in the menagerie, and the same evening he was duly

African and Indian elephant.

packed off to Breslau in charge of a keeper who had assisted in his education. I heard that my pupil in no way disgraced me at the show, but performed his part to the satisfaction of all concerned.

When during the seventies of last century I was exhibiting my great Nubian caravan in the Zoological Gardens at Berlin, there were, among the other visitors from the Dark Continent, five newly imported young African elephants. These youthful monsters stood about five to five and a half feet in height. One day Professor Virchow came to see me, and re-

marked that it would be a great triumph if I could succeed in
training these animals, for at that time it was still erroneously
supposed that the African, unlike the Indian, species of elephant was unfit either for a beast of burden or for a play-actor.
Great was Virchow's astonishment, not to say incredulity,
when I replied that if he cared to come again the following
afternoon he should find the young elephants properly broken
in, notwithstanding the fact that as yet no attempt had been
made to train them. I said that I would teach the brutes to
allow the Nubians to ride them, and also to carry loads. The
professor shook his head sceptically, but promised to come
with some friends the next day at 5 P.M.

There was no time to be lost, for I wished to keep my
word at all costs. No sooner had Virchow departed than
the training was begun. I had the elephants brought out,
and, selecting some of the most agile Nubians, I promised
them rewards if they would clamber on to the elephants' backs
and maintain themselves in that precarious position. The
natives were quite game, but the elephants by no means
relished the part they were expected to play. They found
the loads on their backs uncomfortable, and rushing around
with loud trumpeting, they shook themselves with such
vigour that all the riders except one were sent flying into the
sand. After the animals had been fed with bread and
turnips they became somewhat quieter, and then the
Nubians essayed their task once more, this time with greater
success. This procedure was continued until nightfall, by
which time three of the creatures had been so far broken in
that they would quite good-naturedly allow their native
keepers to ride them about the menagerie. The next morning their good example was followed by their two comrades,
and it now only remained to teach them to carry loads instead of men. I ordered some sacks to be filled and bound
together in pairs with straps, and these were then hung over
the backs of the elephants. The beasts at first disliked the
feeling of the loads resting against their flanks, but they soon

became accustomed to this sensation also. By exhorting, caressing and constantly feeding them with dainties I achieved my object by midday. The African elephants would carry loads, and would allow themselves to be ridden. Professor Virchow arrived at five o'clock with some friends from the Geographical Society and was not a little astonished to see the wild elephants changed into domestic animals after a few hours' schooling.

In 1868 some of my elephants were overtaken by a sad

African elephants.

fate. I had just arrived home from Trieste with a very large collection of animals hailing from Africa. The journey, including a two days' halt in Vienna, had lasted nine days, and both men and beasts were thoroughly exhausted. By the time I had seen all my creatures safely lodged in their respective abodes it was already late in the evening, and I was glad to be able to take myself off to bed without further delay. Among the other animals there were several young elephants, and although these, like all the rest, were very fatigued, they seemed to be quite well, and after taking their food they immediately lay down to sleep. The poor brutes had stood in a very confined space in the railway van, and had had scarcely any rest on the journey.

In the middle of the night, perhaps about two o'clock, my old keeper awoke me with the news that one of the elephants was making a rattling noise in its throat and seemed to be ill. I was somewhat alarmed and intended to go and investigate the matter ; but my fatigue overcame me and I went to sleep again. An hour later another keeper knocked and brought a similar piece of information ; this time I roused myself and was in the stables in a few minutes. But I was too late. One elephant was dead and two others lay dying. An examination showed that the soles of the feet of the dead animal were gnawed through in several places, blood still flowing from the wounds. " Rats," said my old keeper, and so it proved to be, for the marks of their sharp teeth could be plainly recognised in the horny hide, and the dying elephants had similar injuries. Who could have foreseen such a danger? One can only learn these things from experience. There was wooden flooring in the stable, and under these planks the rats had made their nests. The next morning we slew nearly sixty of the assassins, and, I need hardly say, the wooden flooring was promptly removed.

Many large animals are killed by rats. In the Zoological Gardens at Cologne two ostriches were killed by rats during the night. Once, too, fourteen rare Australian parrots belonging to my father were killed by rats at Spielbudenplatz in a single night.

There is no universal rule for the treatment of wild animals. Even individuals of the same species, so great is their variability of temperament, have to be managed according to the particular circumstances of each case. This peculiarity is found, as my narrative has already shown, among elephants. It exists, in a greater or less degree, among all animals, and is a feature in his profession which no successful trainer can overlook.

Moreover, it is difficult to foresee how animals will behave

11 *

under any given circumstances, for they are swayed almost completely by the impulses of the moment, and it frequently happens that an occurrence, to us apparently trifling, will cause a perfectly quiet and well-behaved animal to become almost mad with terror. It is for this reason that presence of mind is an essential quality for the animal trainer to possess ; for he must be ready at all times to grapple with any dangerous whim which, without the slightest apparent cause, may be hatched out in the half-developed intellect of his formidable charge. Nor is it ever easy to convey to the creature's intelligence what is required of him, or to make him understand that what to him appears terrifying, is in reality perfectly harmless.

Suppose, for instance, that one wishes to induce a rhinoceros to walk across a gangway from a ship to the quay, it is not enough to say, " Please, dear Mr. Rhinoceros, will you be so kind as to walk across these planks," for the great herbivore will fail to understand such language, and the most exaggerated politeness will leave him totally unmoved. Even if one places a cord round his neck, and tries to haul him across the bridge, a friend meanwhile prodding him from behind with a stick, the great beast will in all probability refuse to do what is required (for the language of physical force is a dead language to him, be it shouted never so loudly), preferring as an alternative to charge his puny tormentors, and trample them under his feet. But there is one weak spot in the pachyderm's composition, of which his crafty keeper is not slow to make use. He obeys, if not his master, the cravings of his own stomach. The indulgence of appetite establishes a cosmopolitan language, if I may be allowed to call it so, which every animal comprehends. Hold a handful of food to his nose and he will follow wherever you lead him. So it is, at least, with the rhinoceros. Only do this, and all other forms of polite persuasion become superfluous and unnecessary.

These observations recall to my mind a somewhat dangerous adventure which I had in the year 1871, at which time

I possessed no great experience in managing these animals.
William Jamrach had arrived in London from India, with a
number of elephants, rhino-
ceroses and other animals,
which I was to take over. I
went to London to receive
them. Among the other
animals there was a large
female rhinoceros, full-grown,
being seven or eight years
of age. The animal was
housed in an immense cage
built upon the deck. As this
could not be removed, it
was necessary to find some

William Jamrach.

method of transferring the rhinoceros from the ship to the van
provided to convey her to the stable where she was to be
temporarily lodged. The difficulty to be overcome lay in the
distance which separated the ship from the van, a space of about
500 yards. Jamrach suggested that, as the animal was well
behaved, it would be safe to lead her along the docks ; and
without sufficiently realising the great danger of this foolhardy
mode of procedure, I acquiesced in the proposal. Moreover,
I believed that we were really dealing with an unusually quiet
animal.

The preparations were soon complete. Two ropes were
firmly bound round the rhinoceros, one being used as a halter
round her neck and the other being attached to one of the
creature's forelegs, whilst a number of other ropes were kept
in reserve in case of accidents. Then we addressed her in
the cosmopolitan language common to man and beasts.
Jamrach's keeper, offering her food from his hand, backed
slowly, while feeding her, across the gangway. The rhinoceros
followed and the whole party moved in the desired direction.
I gave the long rope attached to the halter to six keepers,
and instructed them to pass this through the bars forming the

side of the van as soon as that vehicle was reached, and to fasten the end to the axle, thus preventing the possibility of the rhinoceros beating a sudden retreat. I myself took the other rope, that attached to the foreleg, and straightway commenced the march through the docks, the rhinoceros following quite quietly. The whole affair appeared to be child's play.

All went well until our strange company had nearly reached the van. Then a most untoward event occurred. To my horror I noticed that a locomotive with a goods train was approaching, and it immediately occurred to me that now, at the very last moment, the rhinoceros might take fright at a spectacle no less novel than terrifying. With a speed which only the fear of danger can explain, I sprang to the van, drew the rhinoceros after me, and, the keepers becoming infected with my energy, we had the animal firmly fastened up before the locomotive reached us. The sequel soon showed how fortunate this was. The engine-driver, who had noticed the uncommon rapidity with which we had completed the last part of our journey, played an idiotic practical joke by blowing his steam-whistle to frighten the rhinoceros. This threw the animal into a terrible state of agitation and she commenced to snort with terror. I had just time to secure her other foreleg with the reserve cords, when her excitement at the continuance of the shrill whistle and at the uproar around us upon the quay turned into furious rage, accompanied by desperate attempts to break away out of the van. The first obstacle she encountered was the coachman's box, which was situated high up in front of the van. In a second the brute had her head under this box and sent it flying into the air. It fell with a crash into the road—luckily missing the horses, or the results would have been disastrous. The infuriated rhinoceros next tried to charge through the front of the van. I was now, however, prepared for the emergency, and swinging myself on to the pole of the cart I seized a thick rope and began to thrash the beast between the ears with all my might and main. Surely even a rhinoceros must feel this, I thought! Eventually both I and my unruly friend the rhinoceros got tired, and gradually the formidable creature recovered her senses and became quiet. But our troubles were not yet at an end ; there remained the still more difficult task of getting the animal out of the van. The stable opened on to the street, so that we were able to back the van up to the door. The animal had to come out of the cart backwards, but this was a proceeding it highly objected to, and the obstinate brute refused to budge an inch. Eventually we fastened cords round each of her hind-legs, and then drew the cords through a ring fastened to the wall of the stable, the same thing being done with the halter rope and with the ropes attached to the forelegs, so that we now had the animal to some extent in our power. As we were hauling the brute out of the van, however, she fell once more into a furious rage, and hurled herself against its sides. She was, moreover, further maddened by the excitement of the crowd which had collected around the stable to witness so unusual a scene. Then I went round to the front of the van and vigorously belaboured the rhinoceros with a cudgel ; this had the desired effect, and we were at last able to get the rebellious monster into the stable. This was the last time I ever transported a rhinoceros in such a manner. I had had enough of the experiment. For the journey to Hamburg I caused an immense cage to be constructed, in which the animal was not nearly so troublesome. This incident will show the reader what sort of difficulties we have to encounter when transporting wild beasts. The adventure might have had a very serious termination.

Besides the common Indian rhinoceros and the African rhinoceros, *Rhinoceros bicornis*, I received towards the end of the seventies the genuine Javan rhinoceros, *Rhinoceros sondaiicus*. In addition, on four different occasions the black Sumatran rhinoceros came into my possession, although with this latter animal I have always had very bad luck, for all the five specimens which I purchased died of enteritis. Unlike the Indian rhinoceros, which is always captured young—

after the mother has been driven off or killed—and brought
up on milk, the Sumatran rhinoceros is taken in pitfalls. This
species is often captured, but in captivity the animals are very
liable to die of the same complaint that killed off all my specimens. There is a representative of this kind of rhinoceros
living in the Imperial Zoological Gardens at Schönbrunn, near
Vienna, and this one is, as far as I know, the only example
which has survived for any length of time in captivity. Another
rarity is the form *Rhinoceros lasiotis*, of which there was about
thirty years ago an example housed in the London Zoological
Gardens, where it lived for more than twenty years. The
common Indian rhinoceros and also the African rhinoceros
thrive excellently in captivity and in our climate ; I know
several of these animals which have lived for more than thirty
years in Zoological Gardens. They are also possessed of
great vitality. On several occasions I have known rhinoceroses break off their horns, without being in any way injured ; the horn soon grows again, and in the course of a year
reaches quite a considerable size.

When they are young, rhinoceroses are very easy to tame.
The young animals which I formerly received from the
Egyptian Sudan were led loose through the desert, it being
found unnecessary to fasten them up in any way. After their
arrival in the laager they became speedily accustomed to
their black keeper, and would follow him about like dogs.
In the Nubian collection which I brought to the Berlin Zoological Gardens in the seventies there were three of these
young rhinoceroses, and I used to allow them to run about
loose, much to the amusement of the public. Great was the
delight of the visitors when the keeper hid himself for a
joke, and the animals, uttering plaintive cries, began to search
for him.

It was some forty years ago that the first rhinoceros
was brought to Europe by my traveller, Cassanova. I
went to Trieste to take it over. I paid £800 down for it,
being under the impression that I had thereby made a very

good bargain. My hopes proved to be illusory, however, for after much discussion the Zoological Society of London, from whom I had expected to obtain a very high price, refused to give me more than £1,000, and even this sum they only offered me under the condition that I should deliver the animal in their Gardens in a good state of health. I did not even receive the purchase-money in hard cash, but to the extent of half the sum had to accept other animals in exchange for my rhinoceros, so that altogether I cleared very little profit out of the transaction.

Young rhinoceros on board ship.

I remember this rhinoceros well, for he came near to doing me a nasty injury. He was quite a young animal and stood only about thirty-two inches at the shoulder, but nevertheless he blossomed out one day into a veritable athlete, a fact which I remember the more because he challenged me to a match, in which no doubt I should have come off second best had I not thought discretion the better part of valour. On the journey from Trieste to Vienna I travelled in the same compartment with the young rhinoceros, for, thinking him to be a very especial treasure, I wished to take charge of him personally. I was dozing comfortably in a corner, when I was suddenly awakened by a pull, and saw that the young rhinoceros had the tail of my coat in his mouth and was cheerfully sucking away at it. The animal appeared to find the flavour pleasant, but the operation not being precisely beneficial to my garment, I endeavoured, with all due politeness, to free the coat from the young herbivore's jaws. The brute, however, was not disposed to submit to this privation; he flew suddenly into a terrific rage, gave a shrill cry of anger, and assaulted me with fury. I fully admit that I was not

over-anxious for a duel with the little monster, and indeed I
found the situation far from pleasant.  With quite remarkable
agility I leaped over boxes and sacks to escape from the
formidable onset, and in so doing I upset a sack weighing
about 150 lb., which rolled into the rhinoceros's stall ; and
the animal, possibly mistaking the harmless sack for his
enemy, hurled it into the air as though it had been an india-
rubber ball.  Not wishing to give our African guest any
opportunity of playing catch-ball with me, after the manner of
his game with the sack, I hastily changed my quarters and
completed the journey in safety.  Later, when I was taking
this young rhinoceros to London, I had further proof of his
violent disposition.  Being annoyed by the movements of his
cage while it was being taken ashore, he charged the wall and
split the thick planks as though they had been no stronger
than the wood of a cigar box.  I then, however, covered the
entire cage in a cloth, which put the animal in darkness and
thus quieted him, and he eventually arrived safely at his
destination.

The hippopotamus is an even more bulky animal than its
relative the rhinoceros ; but nevertheless one of my travellers
on one occasion actually transported a specimen in an ordin
ary travelling trunk.  The story no doubt sounds slightly improbable and may perhaps remind the reader of the American
commercial traveller who journeyed with his trunk full—so he
asserted—of telegraph poles !  Yet on this occasion I am not
trying to presume upon the credulity of the public.  Curiously
enough there occurred a considerable time ago an illustration
in a German comic journal—which is here reproduced—representing a traveller for my firm exhibiting samples of various
animals, all packed in this very fashion.  The artist might
well be alluding to the incident of which I am here speaking,
for I did really receive a hippopotamus packed up as ordinary
luggage.  The keeper whom I sent to Bordeaux to receive
the animal transported it simply in a large travelling trunk,
which he registered to Hamburg as luggage !  The beast

was a female hailing from the west coast of Africa, and weighed, it is true, only eighty pounds. The trunk, with its unusual contents, was delivered safely in Hamburg, and the hippopotamus is now to be seen in the Zoological Gardens at Hanover.

It does not do to play with these great animals, for, like rhinoceroses, they are liable to violent fits of ill temper and are then extremely dangerous. Indeed, they are (as I have previously remarked when describing the methods of capturing the beasts) much less tractable than rhinoceroses, and do not

" My name is Schmidt. I am travelling for the firm of Hagenbeck. Permit me to show you my samples."

usually conceive that strong affection for their keepers which is so commonly to be observed in the case of the latter animals. The transport of these creatures is often a most difficult, not to say dangerous, operation. I once had an adventure with a female hippopotamus, much resembling the little incident with the rhinoceros at the London docks. It occurred about twenty-five years ago. I had just purchased the hippopotamus in question in South Germany, and on the animal's arrival at Hamburg it was, of course, necessary to transfer it from the waggon to the stable which was to be its home. The usual method of procedure—the cosmopolitan language—was first tried, but the lady, having not only a thick hide but also a thick head, obstinately refused to come out. She merely approached the door, and snapped at the delicacies offered her, then retired once more into the waggon. This sort of foolery continued for several hours, until at last I lost all patience with the brute and ordered two of my people, whilst I once more enticed her to the door with a handful of food, to belabour her from the rear. Seeing the food, the cow once again came to the door, but on being hit from behind, instead of coming right out, she turned round in a fury, and charged the barrier dividing her from her assailants with such force that this gave way and fell with a crash, burying the two keepers beneath it. The hippopotamus was about to follow up her advantage, when I sprang to the rescue and gave her a tremendous kick with my right foot. The result of this was to turn her attention to myself, and with a snort of rage she came at me with a rush. I ran—ran as I had never run before—and fled into the stable prepared for the hippopotamus, the infuriated beast following with wide-open jaws. Springing across the bath, I made my escape through the bars, which were very wide apart—but only just in time! Outside, I rushed round to the door of the stall and quickly closed it—the hippopotamus was secured! I have always regretted that there was no photographic—or better, cinematographic—camera on the spot to preserve the doubtless highly comical sight of my panic-stricken flight from the hippopotamus cow.

Hippopotami thrive excellently in captivity and have bred in many Zoological Gardens, among others in London, Amsterdam, Antwerp and St. Petersburg. The act of mating takes place in the water, the animals becoming sexually mature in the fifth year. It is a pretty sight to see the mother playing in the water with her baby, or, when the little one is tired, giving it a ride upon her back. As I have said, the animals are usually somewhat bad tempered throughout their lives and are apt to be irritable, but of course the

characters of different individuals vary. They sometimes become quite tame. I remember a pair of full-grown hippopotami which I saw in a circus in America, and which were
as gentle and well behaved as could possibly be desired.
The American circuses are in the habit of carrying out great
parades through the streets, and on such occasions these two
hippopotami used to walk quite loose by the side of their
keeper, nor did any accident ever occur.

The other species of the genus *Hippopotamus* is the dwarf
hippopotamus, which inhabits Liberia. In the sixties a young
specimen of this animal, which weighed not quite thirty pounds,
was taken to Dublin, but it survived only a few weeks. This
was the only representative of the dwarf hippopotamus which
has ever been brought to Europe.

The last of the giant herbivores whose ways in captivity
I have to describe is the giraffe. There is probably no
animal which created such a stir when first brought to Europe
as did the giraffe. Now that the beast is such a common
inmate of Zoological Gardens that many town-bred lads are
more familiar with it than they are with cows or pigs, it
is difficult to realise the astonishment of the public when
they first saw this grotesque creature, looking like Gulliver
among the Lilliputians. It may readily be imagined that
when these ungulates first arrived in Europe they caused no
little embarrassment to their owners; for instance, if they
were not to be left out of doors at night some stable must
be found in which to house them—but where and how it
was difficult to see, for all the stables available were too small
and too low. Even when this obstacle has been overcome,
and stables high enough have been provided, the animals are
still liable to a peculiar and painful kind of accident. The
giraffe's long neck is no doubt highly advantageous to the
creature in the wild state—for, as is well known, it is thereby
enabled to reach a plentiful supply of the leaves of trees upon
which it feeds—but in captivity it is apt to prove a very
awkward possession. One morning in the summer of 1876

three of my giraffes were found lying helpless on the ground, still living it is true, but all with broken necks. The stable was high and wide enough, yet evidently the animals must have driven their heads against the walls, perhaps during a rumpus, and in that way broken the fragile cervical vertebræ. On two other occasions I experienced similar misfortunes,

Giraffes.

and of course in all cases there was nothing to be done but at once to put an end to the poor beasts.

Young giraffes are liable to be attacked by a peculiar disease, which is in all probability connected with the change of food that they undergo during their period of acclimatisation. The knees become swollen, and the animals eventually become bandy-legged and lame in their forelegs, and as a rule die within a year. Occasionally, however, they do recover; for example, there is now living in one of the Duke of Bedford's English parks a giraffe which three years ago was affected with the disease. Although the precise cause of this ailment has not as yet been definitely ascertained, the trouble has now been overcome, for we have adopted a new method of feeding which appears to keep the animals immune from its attacks. At all events, since then, we have lost no more specimens from this cause.

Giraffes in general are certainly not delicate animals. Various menageries, among others that of the elder Kreutzberg, have travelled about for years with giraffes, the beasts apparently suffering in no way from their wandering life. A specimen, which I sold to Barnum, withstood the hardships of travelling in a tent circus for as long as eight years, and would undoubtedly have lived much longer still, if it had not been killed in an accident. Furthermore, these long-legged mammals will breed very readily in captivity; to my knowledge, they have done so in the Zoological Gardens in London, Paris, Berlin, Vienna, Amsterdam, and Hamburg, the most recent births being in London, Berlin and Cologne.

The first giraffes that were ever seen in Europe were sent over by the Viceroy of Egypt in the summer of 1827 as gifts to the British and French Governments, and were lodged in the London Zoological Gardens and in the Jardin des Plantes at Paris. For some years after this there were not very many giraffes imported, only an occasional example arriving in Europe, but later on, especially during the decade 1867-1877, the number brought from the Sudan was very large. In the year 1876 I myself received no fewer than thirty-five specimens, and I, of course, was not the only importer. There was, for instance, another firm which exported from Africa twenty-six specimens. The result of this was that the price for these "goods" sunk deplorably, and it became necessary to decrease the importation. A year later I sold the last three young giraffes in my stock to an Englishman for the ridiculous price of £150. Not long after this, the excessive importation of these creatures was put a stop to by the outbreak of the war against the Mahdi, but unfortunately, as the reader already knows, it became at the same time almost impossible to capture any other animals whatsoever in that part of Africa.

# CHAPTER VII.

## REPTILES IN CAPTIVITY.

THERE is no class of animal that excites such general dislike as snakes. Rudyard Kipling has well expressed the universal abhorrence of these creatures in the story of Mogli in the subterranean vaults of the rattle-snake, when he wished to have nothing to do with the "poison people". They are a friendless and isolated group; and in all parts of the world every man's hand is turned against them.

On one occasion—it was the summer of 1874—I well remember the commotion that ensued in my menagerie when a gigantic snake escaped from its cage. The reptile was a somewhat feeble specimen of python, which had recently arrived from Africa in poor condition. It had been ordered a warm bath, and for this purpose had been conveyed to a tub which stood in the carnivore house. The tub had a lid, over which was a cloth cover, so that when once the animal had been inserted there seemed little danger of its escaping. But escape it did. After I had seen it comfortably stowed away in the tub I went to my office to do some writing. About a couple of hours later I was startled by the alarming news that the snake had escaped and was at that very moment crawling about among the cages of the apes and parrots, which in those early days found their abode in the carnivore house. I ran quickly to the spot, and the confusion which I found there would be difficult to describe. Every animal in the carnivore house without exception was in a state of abject terror. They could see nothing and think of nothing but the escaped reptile. The lions, panthers, and other great

beasts were springing about their cages as though they had
suddenly gone mad, dashing themselves against the bars with
loud roaring or mewing. The apes and parrots were shriek-
ing, so that the din was hideous.

To catch the snake was no easy matter. Its warm bath
had given it so much vitality that for a long time it eluded
all our efforts to capture it. In vain did we throw a cloth
over it; each time it quickly wriggled out from underneath and
we had to pursue it again. At last we got a net which I
often used for taking monkeys or small carnivores out of their
cages, and this we threw over the serpent's head. He bit
savagely at it and soon made large holes in it; but the
manœuvre gave me time to grip him by the back of the neck,
and very shortly, with the help of several keepers, and by
exerting our utmost strength, we got him safely packed into
the net and transferred to a secure cage. The excitement in
the carnivore house gradually subsided, and peace reigned
there once more.

The apprehension excited among the animals by the
escape of this reptile points to an instinct which is very valuable to them in wild nature. For no animal is more dangerous, none requires to be treated with greater caution, than a
snake. With the poisonous kinds, this is readily understood;
but even the non-poisonous kinds, especially when large,
are very dangerous, for they possess prodigious muscular
strength and bite fiercely whenever they are irritated. They
are exceedingly ferocious. Of the many animals which at one
time or another have endangered my life, snakes have been
the sinners much the most frequently. Often as I have been
bitten or scratched by various animals, I have suffered far more
from snakes than from anything else. I have known many
thousands of them and acquired an intimate knowledge of their
habits and disposition. I have even had to fight with them
almost as in a wrestling match. It is said that in Borneo the
natives are frequently attacked and devoured by giant
serpents, and from what I have seen of their capacity for

dealing with large prey I have no doubt that a full-grown Borneo python could easily swallow a man. Any snake of from eighteen to twenty feet long is strong enough to squeeze a man to death if only it can get him properly encircled in its coils.

Some years ago a controversy was started in the English newspapers as to what length snakes might run to. It was alleged that there were kinds which reached thirty or forty feet, and one traveller offered to produce one in support of his statement if anybody would pay £500 for it. As I happened to know that the largest snake ever seen was only twenty-six feet long, I thought I was justified in entering into this controversy; and through the agency of my English friends I offered not £500 but £1,000 to any one who should bring to Hamburg a live and healthy snake thirty feet long. Up to the present time no such snake has arrived.

The voracity of snakes is quite extraordinary. Until lately I had been accustomed to feed these creatures on fairly small animals, but a short time ago I gave to one of my Borneo giants a Chinese dwarf hog weighing fully fifty pounds, and this was demolished by the serpent in three-quarters of an hour. Soon after I had a further exhibition of the gastronomic capacity of snakes. On this occasion the creature was an extremely large one, about twenty-five feet long. I gave him a goat weighing thirty-one

After dinner.

pounds which I thought would provide him with a pretty hearty meal, but he made nothing of it. A few hours later he swallowed a buck of forty-three pounds which had been refused by three other snakes, the swallowing process being completed in half an hour. But even this did not satisfy his appetite. About a week later I had to destroy a Siberian goat weighing fifty-two pounds, and after cutting off the horns, I threw the carcase into the reptile's den. Neither I nor the keeper imagined that the snake would be able to swallow so large an animal; but when I returned an hour later I found that it had already been partially swallowed, the head being half-way down the monster's throat. I quickly sent for a photographer, and by the time he arrived half the goat had already disappeared. The effort of swallowing was evidently very great. From time to time the snake emitted deep groans such as I had never heard before; but slowly the prey continued to vanish. When only a small part of the hind quarters was left projecting from the serpent's jaws I had the photograph taken. A minute after, the snake, which had been swallowing its victim for two hours, brought it all up again. Whether it had been frightened by the process of photographing, or whether it had taxed its powers too severely, I cannot say.

With a view to discovering the effects upon the animal which had been swallowed and then brought up again, I had it dissected on the following day. It was found that the goat's neck had been twisted completely out of its articulations. The ribs had been so pressed that they had all broken off from the vertebræ. From this, some idea can be obtained of the immense strength of these great creatures.

Snakes do not begin to swallow their prey until they have killed it, which usually takes them a very short time. They always make for the head, and with lightning rapidity coil round the body of their prey. They then seize the head in their jaws and wring the animal's neck. They keep firm hold upon the animal until the absence of any movement shows that it is quite dead. The feast then commences. In the case of large animals the snake first of all covers the head with saliva so as to make it easy to swallow. It then encircles the animal with its tail-end and gradually presses it downwards into its mouth, at the same time moving its jaws to and fro. In swallowing, the snake's jaws distend like an india-rubber bag, and to an extent which, unless seen, appears incredible. Now and then the snake will pause for as long as ten or twelve minutes for a rest. These pauses I particularly noticed in the case of the reptile swallowing the Siberian goat as above recorded. Since this incident I have seen a case even more remarkable, in which another snake devoured a goat weighing ninety-three pounds in about an hour and a half.

When one looks through the glass fronts of their cages and sees them apparently so lazy and devoid of vitality, it is difficult to imagine the great strength and swiftness which all these animals possess. In spite of the great precautions which one always has to take in dealing with snakes, there still remains a considerable element of danger when anything has to be done with them. I have had many hundreds of giant snakes through my hands, in the most literal sense, in the course of my life, and have often been bitten by them. It is, however, not the bite of these large creatures that is most to be feared, but their powerful muscular coils.

A very serious adventure, in which the reptiles appeared in all their native savagery, occurred at Stellingen in the early summer of 1904. We were preparing to pack up four great specimens of the species *Python reticulatus*, varying in length from twenty to twenty-six feet, to be sent to the St. Louis Exhibition. My son Heinrich, having made all the necessary preparations, went to open the door of the cage, but no sooner had he opened it than the four reptiles, as though by a prearranged plan, flew at him with wide-open jaws. One of them very nearly succeeded in coiling itself round him in spite of his efforts, and if it had succeeded his death would have been

a certainty. But he defended himself vigorously, and I myself and a keeper running to his aid, helped him with all our
strength in his struggle against the monster. But it was some
minutes before we finally succeeded in freeing him. The others
we secured with some little difficulty by the aid of the usual
woollen coverings and sacks ; but even this was accomplished
only at the cost of much time and some danger. The largest
of them, a savage monster weighing quite 200 lb., took up his
position on a rafter at the top of the cage and fixed himself
there firmly with his tail-end, while with his head-end he made
savage bites at his opponents. When once we had thrown
the sack over his head our next proceeding was to unloosen
the tail-end which was tightly fixed to the rafter. We had to
secure further assistance to muster the strength necessary for
this purpose. But even then the fight was not over. No
sooner had we, with great effort, got the tail-end loose than
the monster got it twisted round Heinrich's right leg, and with
irresistible force began to twine itself higher and higher up his
body. It was indeed a life-and-death struggle which then ensued, but by exerting all our might we at last succeeded in
tearing away the reptile and forcing it into a sack. The work
of overpowering these four monsters was one that I shall not
easily forget.

Skill in dealing with these dangerous animals can only be
obtained by dint of many experiments, some of which are
successful and others not. I remember one episode which
helped me to acquire some experience of my own. In the
early seventies a ship coming from Brazil brought to Hamburg a couple of boa-constrictors. When I went on board
for the purpose of looking at them, the steward told me that
they were lying inanimate in their cage and were certainly
dead. On inspecting the animals it appeared that the
steward's estimate was correct. They had been kept all night
in an open cage in the captain's cabin ; and, although it was
the middle of December, no sort of heating or shelter from
the cold had been attempted. The snakes had in fact been

frozen. The captain, who arrived at the moment and saw the lifeless condition of the creatures, ordered them to be thrown overboard. I requested, however, to be allowed to make an attempt to revive them, and, having received the captain's permission, wrapt them in a rug and carried them off. I took them home to our house in Spielbudenplatz, and there shook them out on the floor; but my father was as incredulous as the captain with regard to the possibility of bringing them to life. Nevertheless I thought I would make the experiment, so I laid the two snakes in front of the stove which was situated in our aviary and went upstairs to my own rooms. After about an hour a violent commotion took place among the birds, and on running downstairs I found the spot before the stove deserted and the two reptiles taking a constitutional round the room. As I was trying to secure them a strange coincidence occurred. The door opened and in walked old Kreutzberg, who had just arrived from Russia, and wished to purchase some snakes for his menagerie. With his help the animals were quickly secured, and, ten minutes later, they had passed into the possession of Kreutzberg for a sum of eighty Prussian thalers (£12). Thus there came an unexpected windfall to two persons—to my father, who in the afternoon heard that the dead snakes had come to life again and were sold for a good price, and to the captain, who received next day an unexpected forty thalers as his share in the transaction.

In the course of further experience I have learnt that it is no uncommon thing for snakes to come to life again in this remarkable manner, but there is a limit beyond which their endurance cannot be taxed. I remember a case in point, which occurred in March 1883, when I had purchased in England 165 giant serpents for a figure exceeding £1,000. The snakes were shipped from London to Hamburg, but, as ill-luck would have it, a severe north-easterly gale was encountered during the crossing, and the vessel had to put back to Gravesend for the purpose of recoaling. At last she

started again, but it was seven days before the snakes arrived
in Hamburg; and at that time of year seven days on the
North Sea is naturally a great strain upon animals accustomed
to tropical climates.    I had a premonition that the affair would
turn out badly, and so it happened ; for on their arrival at
Hamburg the whole collection were dead.    I hastened with
them to my establishment and applied all known means of
revivifying them, but in vain.    It was too late.    Not one was
saved.    When I mention that I lost over this transaction not
only the £1,000 paid for the snakes, but a great deal more
for which I had already sold them in advance to America, it
will be readily understood that my sorrow at the affair was
genuine.

If the non-poisonous snakes are dangerous, the poisonous
snakes are, of course, much more so.    In handling these I am
always uncommonly careful, and whenever any of them reach
my establishment among a collection of animals, I always
pass them on to their next destination as quickly as circumstances will permit.    The first adventure which I had with
the "poison people" was in the sixties, when a case of puff-
adders arrived for us and was brought to the house.    The
case was a large flat one, made of wire netting covered round
with wooden boards.    It was impossible to keep them in this
case, and I was therefore confronted with the problem of
changing them into a new one.    I thought I should be able
simply to shake them out from the old cage into the new ;
and with this intent I tore away a portion of the side of the
old cage.    But they were not to be transferred so easily.
They darted to the opening, but instead of passing over into
the other cage they endeavoured to get away sideways.
Nothing could persuade them to go into the new cage, and
at one moment two of the reptiles very nearly escaped.    I
was so horrified at this possibility that I gingerly shook them
back into the old cage and pressed the new one against
the opening so as to block it up.    I then with some little
difficulty managed to fasten up again the hole which I had

made. I had by this time had enough of the job for one day, and the next day when I applied myself to the task once more I devised a new plan for effecting the change. I tore off the boards which surrounded the wire netting in the old cage, and in the wire netting itself I bored a small four-cornered hole, against which I placed the opening of the new cage—an opening which was capable of being closed by means of a sliding door. The new cage was in darkness; and the old cage, now that the boards had been removed from it, was flooded with light. Now it is a peculiarity of snakes that they all like to crawl away into the darkest corners they can find ; and after an hour all the puff-adders, eight in number, had gone across into the new cage. I then merely closed the sliding door and the transference had been effected. Since that time, when they so nearly escaped, I have always had a holy horror of poisonous snakes.

The bite of a rattle-snake is exceedingly poisonous ; and I have observed that white rats given them for food usually die within half a minute of being bitten. This is, however, by no means invariable. Under natural conditions out of doors it sometimes happens that the weak and unprotected creature will overcome one much more powerful and better armed. I have known a case in which a rattle-snake was killed by a rat given it for food. The rat was put in the cage one evening, and when we came round next morning we found the rattle-snake lying dead, and the rat sitting triumphantly in a corner of the cage. He had even commenced to make a meal off the body of the formidable reptile. An examination of the marks upon the dead snake's body showed that the rat must have sprung suddenly upon the nape of its neck and, having planted its teeth firmly there, held on tightly until the rattle-snake died. A large piece had been taken out of the animal's neck which the rat had devoured. After this experience we never again used wild rats as food for snakes.

Fights between snakes for food are not uncommon, and in the course of these fights it very often happens that the

larger snake will swallow not only the food but the smaller
snake also at the same time.    Snakes are guilty of a senseless,
one might almost say mechanical, gluttony.    Of this I had
interesting evidence in an episode which occurred near the beginning of the seventies, when we were still at Spielbudenplatz.    At that place we kept our snakes in large dark cages
heated from below by hot-water pipes.    We used, moreover,
to keep the animals wrapt up in rugs, which were only removed
when they were being fed.    One day we received a boa-con-
strictor about eleven feet long—a very large size for this
species, of which (contrary to the popular idea) I have never
seen a specimen of more than thirteen feet.    Immediately on
his arrival I gave him a large rabbit, which he ate during the
night.    Thinking that he had had enough for the present I
gave him nothing the next night, but left him as usual wrapt up
in the rug.    He apparently mistook the rug for food, for he
attempted to swallow it.    When I came next morning I found
half the rug down the animal's throat.    The animal itself was
suffocated and quite dead.

I have never again come across an instance of so strange
a death, but I have often lost snakes through their savage
fights for prey.    About ten years ago I gave a rabbit to a
couple of yellow pythons, one nine feet and the other seven
feet long.    The next morning I found that the nine-foot
python had swallowed not only the rabbit but the seven-foot
python as well.    From later observation I infer that both
snakes must have attacked the rabbit at the same time, one
at the head and the other at the tail.    Both then proceeded
to swallow the rabbit from opposite ends, and in this way the
smaller snake was swallowed as a sort of continuation of the
rabbit by the larger one.    I could easily see on the following
morning the outline of the smaller, in the body of the larger
snake.

The power of digestion possessed by snakes is perfectly
extraordinary.    The most remarkable case of heavy feeding
which has come under my observation occurred about ten

Snake gnawed by a rat.

years ago at Neuer Pferdemarkt, when an Indian python, only fourteen feet long, swallowed four lambs within twenty-four hours, each weighing from twelve to nineteen pounds and possessing horns several inches long. After this performance the snake was so swollen by the gas evolved in its interior by the semi-digested lambs that it burst open for a length of about a foot, the two edges yawning apart to a width of a couple of inches. This meal took about ten days to digest, and on the eleventh day the snake took another lamb. The woollen parts were thrown out in compact balls; whilst the horns and hoofs passed through the snake's body unchanged.

Ten days is a comparatively brief period for the digestion of its food by a snake. I remember the case of a giant serpent which had eaten a hog; the signs of digestion actually did not commence for four weeks and were not completed until ten weeks later. That pigs are found by snakes rather hard to digest I have other evidence. Some time ago two very large Borneo snakes arrived at my garden, having accomplished safely a long voyage direct from Singapore. One of them was twenty-five feet long and weighed 248 lbs. I concluded from their savageness that they had not been in captivity very long, and in this belief I was justified a week later by finding among their excrement the tusks and hoofs of a wild boar. This must have been food which they had caught when still in a state of freedom.

Correlated with the capacity for consuming enormous quantities of food is the capacity for going for long periods without any food at all. In the wild state it must often happen that snakes for many weeks together are unable to catch any prey that is suitable to them, and hence it is necessary for their preservation that when they do catch food they shall be able to consume it in large quantities. Animals in captivity, which have taken their food regularly week by week, will suddenly cease to take it and fast for more than six months. In the Zoological Gardens at Amsterdam the former director, Dr. Westermann, who has now been dead

for a long time, recorded the case of a snake which ate nothing for two whole years, but then began to take food quite
cheerfully again and lived for many years afterwards in the
Gardens.    This animal was a Brazilian water-snake, *Eunectes
murinus.*

I myself have had a very similar experience.    On this
occasion the animal was a dark Indian python about sixteen
feet long, which was in very good condition when it came
into my hands, but would eat nothing and fasted for a period
of two years and a month.    During this time it drank large
quantities of water, but the effects of starvation soon became
apparent.    The creature shrank until it was little more than
a skeleton of skin and bones.    After this long period I
thought it time to intervene.    So I took a pigeon and moist-
ened it in warm water ; and then, seizing the python by the
nape of the neck, I opened its jaws and forced the pigeon
down its throat for a distance of about a foot.    The rest the
snake managed for itself, and one could see the pigeon
gradually slipping down the reptile's body.    With eating the
creature showed signs of returning appetite.    That same evening I placed a live pigeon in the cage, and the snake after a
short time killed and began to devour it.    But its strength was
so exhausted that it was unable to swallow the bird unaided ;
and I had to assist by using a sort of ramrod, with which I
slowly pushed the pigeon down the python's throat.    We
then left another pigeon in the cage, but the remedy had been
applied too late, and the next morning we found the snake
lying dead with the pigeon in its jaws.    It had expired in
attempting to swallow its prey.

Snakes eat most readily in bright weather and will seldom
touch anything when the air is oppressive.    The most important point in their management is to secure proper warmth and
ventilation in their cages.    The temperature should not be
permitted to fall below 72° F. and may well be a few degrees
higher.    If a proper temperature is not provided, the snakes
refuse to eat and they catch colds, which take the form of a

scurvy of the mouth. All that it is necessary to do under these circumstances is to place them in a warm cage with a large water bath, in which they will lie for weeks with only the tips of their noses above the surface. The water has a cura‑ tive effect upon the mouth, the purulent parts becoming loosened so that the reptiles can shake them off, and in this way snakes have been cured in which large pieces of the jaws had already been eaten away.

A good deal is yet to be learnt with regard to the breed‑ ing of snakes; but I am looking forward to making some ex‑ periments in this line during the next few years at my animal park at Stellingen. Young snakes come into the world in two different ways. The boa-constrictors and other Indian snakes lay eggs and hatch them out. The water-snakes, on the other hand, do not lay eggs but bear living young. About fifteen years ago I had an opportunity of observing the course of events in one of these latter cases. The mother was an *Eunectes murinus*, which is one of the largest species of Brazilian snakes, and is said to attain to as much as twenty feet in length. The one that I possessed was fifteen feet long, and after I had had her a few months she was delivered of a family of forty-eight children. I was unable to take the news to the lucky father, for he had been left behind in the forests of Brazil. But the story had a tragic termination, for they all died on being born. I have also had some ex‑ perience of the oviparous kinds, especially in the case of a certain dark python which had laid an enormous number of eggs. She used to lie coiled around these, and whenever I approached the nest three or four young ones would shoot out their heads angrily at me from among the eggs. Out of a total of about fifty eggs the snake succeeded in hatching twenty-one while the rest became dried up. The young snakes were fond of returning to their egg-shells after they had been born. They used them as nests, and if they came out at all, only did so to crawl round for a few minutes and then return. The feeding was a matter of some difficulty.

They would not touch frogs, but when I put some young white mice into their cage they seized, killed and swallowed them in the same way as the adults do.   Eventually I sold the whole family to the Jardin d'Acclimatisation in Paris, where, however, proper care was not taken of them and they soon died.   They were then stuffed and mounted with their egg-shells; and are still on view for any one who likes to go and see them.

I made another attempt at breeding snakes in the year 1904, when I received indirectly from Singapore a very large *Python reticulatus* which in the course of its journey had laid no fewer than 103 eggs.   Of these eighty-eight were hatched, and I purchased the entire family; but only thirty-three reached me alive, measuring about eighteen inches each.   Some I gave away, others refused their food and died, until at last I had only sixteen individuals left.   These I treated with the utmost possible care, feeding them on sparrows and mice.   At first they seemed to do well, but eventually every one of them died from convulsions.   I think the cause of their illness must have been an insufficient supply of fresh air; for among all living beings fresh air is one of the most essential conditions for the maintenance of good health.   They all died within a few days of each other, and the catastrophe was the more regrettable in that up till that time they had thriven excellently, three already measuring over four feet, and one of these over five feet, in length.

The intelligence of snakes has been in my opinion greatly exaggerated.   It is true that the frequency with which snake-charmers are to be met would seem to indicate a certain degree of educability in the animals; but I should be very sceptical as to the possibility of snakes approaching in this respect any of the higher animals.   I do not think that the snake-charmer can enter into the same friendly relation with his pupils that trainers can do among the apes, ungulates, and carnivores.   Of course they have some capacity for learning tricks, but their main characteristics seem to be gluttony, laziness and an exceedingly bad temper. In this respect I draw no distinction between the different species of snakes; they all seem to me pretty much alike.

Snake-charmers cannot do nearly as much as they pretend and are popularly supposed to do. The common belief that they work with the cobra or Indian spectacled snake is entirely erroneous. It may be true in the case of some of the native Indian snake-charmers, but their European confrères work almost exclusively with the young of the giant serpents, sometimes the Indian python and sometimes the South American boa. The public are so little acquainted with the differences between different kinds of snakes, that they often think that the snake-charmer is handling a very poisonous creature, when in reality the animal belongs to a perfectly harmless species. The charmer does all that he can to encourage this idea, but at the same time he takes very good care never to have anything to do with any poisonous snake, unless or until its

Indian snake-charmer.

poison fangs have been removed. But even then he has to be pretty careful, for the poison fangs grow again, and unless he watches them closely he will run considerable risk. A poison snake from which the fangs have been removed is much more harmless than an ordinary giant snake, even

though quite young; for, the poison fangs being the only
weapons which these creatures possess in nature, they are
wholly disabled by their removal, whereas the non-poisonous
snakes are endowed with other weapons of defence, with
which they can at any time give a good account of themselves.
Their bite is much more severe than that of the poisonous
kinds, and by their habit of coiling round their enemy, a snake
eighteen feet long can squeeze a strong man sufficiently to
put his life in danger from suffocation.

So-called snake tricks are very easily contrived.  As a
rule they consist of nothing more than letting the animal
suddenly out of darkness into a strong light, when it will fly
up in anger and appear to threaten its master.  The display
is then concluded by playing music, with which the snake
seems to be calmed; for snakes, in common with all other
animals, are very sensitive to the effects of music.  I do not
suggest that they would appreciate the Moonlight Sonata as
much as they would a rabbit, but nevertheless it is undeni-
able that they derive real pleasure from listening to music.

As we are now on the subject of venomous snakes I may
take the opportunity of relating a method by which the poison
may be extracted from these animals.  I learnt the method
from a learned Indian, by name Mr. Docton, who was employed at the time in the Zoological Gardens at Bombay.
From a cage of venomous snakes he took out the animals
one by one with the aid of an iron bar twisted at the end into
a hook.  When this hook was placed round the snake's body
the animal could be lifted up by means of it; for the cobra,
which is the common venomous snake of India, and of which
I am here writing, does not possess the power which other
snakes possess of twisting round a smooth rod, but just hangs
loosely from the hook.  Having lifted it out of the cage, Mr.
Docton laid it on the ground, at the same time pinning it
down with a forked stick by the nape of the neck.  The
poison is now extracted by the following method : An assistant brings a mussel shell, of which the concave side is

covered with a green leaf, and places this green leaf immediately in front of the serpent's mouth. By pressing the back
of the animal's neck with the fingers it can be made to open
its jaws and bite deeply into the leaf. When killing their
prey snakes use only a small portion of the poison which
their fangs contain, but when subjected to pressure in the
manner above described, they eject their whole supply, which,
passing through the holes in the leaf made by the bite, collects
in the hollow of the mussel shell beneath. By the employment
of this method it has been found that the collected poison of
a hundred cobras in the dried state amounts to no more than
four grammes. This would be sufficient to kill several hundred
large mammals or several thousand men—so concentrated
and so virulent is the poison. A reptile which has been
deprived of its poison in this manner takes about a week
to renew its supply.

Mr. Docton also made experiments as to the practicability
of conferring immunity from the effects of snake poison by
administering small but gradually increasing injections of the
liquid. On this point he completely established his case.
It was found possible to render monkeys immune within a
period of six months ; and, taking into consideration the well-
known similarity between the reactions of monkeys and men,
there seems no reason to doubt that a similar immunity might
easily be conferred upon human beings. It has not yet been
ascertained whether immunity from the poison of one species
of snake would carry with it immunity from the poisons of all
other species ; but any such general immunity appears improbable, and for the following reason. When two snakes
of the same species attack one another they remain unaffected
by each other's poison, but when the reptiles are of different
species they rapidly succumb to each other's bites. This
statement, which I make on the authority of Mr. Docton
and which I firmly believe to be true, seems to indicate a
great difference in the quality of the poisons of the different
species. The dried snake poison is of a yellowish-green

13 *

colour and is composed of crystalline bodies. It has been
bought chiefly by Dr. Fraser of Edinburgh and Dr. Moeller
of Australia, and I hope before long that the results of their
experiments will be published.

All this that I have related with regard to snakes gives
some colour of truth to many of those Oriental snake stories
which date back several thousand years. There seems no

Indian jugglers.

inherent improbability in the tale of Mithridates the king,
who made himself gradually immune against all the poisons
known in his day by taking slowly increasing quantities of
them. For the same reason I am not inclined to disbelieve
the stories about Indian jugglers who work with venomous
snakes in which the fangs have not been removed. From
their youngest childhood they have been made immune by
the use of snake poison, so that when they have grown up

they suffer no danger even from the bite of an adult cobra with all its poison apparatus in full working order. The saliva of such immune persons is said to act almost like an antitoxin ; and it is related that lives have been saved by rubbing it into the wounds caused by bites. But for the truth of this story I cannot be responsible. I merely set it down for what it may be worth.

Let us pass now from snakes to another kind of reptile no less formidable or repulsive—I mean the crocodile. Since in my youth I was bitten by one of these animals I have always stood in a wholesome fear of them. On this occasion the bite nearly ended in a very serious manner. It did not at first appear to be serious. The crocodile, which was about two feet long, nipped my right hand and I foolishly took no notice of it ; but about three hours afterwards my hand began to swell and the swelling spread up the arm, attended with great pain. I sat up all night washing the wound with ice-cold water and bathing the arm, and on the next morning when I sent for a physician I learned that this treatment alone had probably been instrumental in saving my arm. The swelling slowly disappeared, but the memory of it has remained.

Since that time more than two thousand crocodiles have passed through my hands at one time or another, but I have carefully avoided running the risk of any further accident. On one occasion, however, in spite of my precautions, an incident occurred which nearly cost me my life. I was engaged in packing up twenty alligators to be exhibited at Dusseldorf, among a large collection of other reptiles, in the Zoological Gardens at that place. The alligators were from six to ten feet long, and I was removing them one by one from the basin for the purpose of packing them. As I was taking out the seventh, it suddenly gave me such a terrific blow with its tail that I was precipitated into the water into the very midst of the savage reptiles. The thing happened so quickly that it took the alligators some moments to recover from their surprise, and I took advantage of this brief interval to clamber

with lightning speed out of the basin.   If one of the animals
had attacked me the rest would have followed suit and I
should have been done for.   I know from personal experience
that when these creatures have secured prey, they all seize it
in their jaws and try to tear it away from each other.   My
fate would, indeed, have been unenviable.

Though I myself have never fallen into the clutches of these
animals, I have witnessed them engaging in fights among
themselves of the most savage and merciless description.
When once an alligator has seized an enemy it will not leave
go, even though its head be broken to pieces.   I saw such a
fight in the eighties when we had received a consignment of
nearly 300 alligators, mostly from one to four feet in length, but
including half a dozen which measured from ten to twelve feet.
All these animals, having been kept ever since their capture
in small cages, had become extremely ill tempered, and it was
necessary to observe the utmost caution in dealing with them.
I took the boxes and placed them one by one in the enclosure destined for the reptiles.   When each box had been
placed in the enclosure I tore off the boards at the head-end
of it, and by prodding the animal's tail with a stick induced it
to walk out.   The first alligator walked quietly out of his box
and into the pond ; so did the next three, and all seemed to
be going smoothly.   But as the fifth and sixth were released
they rushed upon one another without any apparent reason
and engaged in a desperate encounter.   In a few minutes the
whole basin was a compact knot of snarling animals biting
savagely at each other and lashing the water wildly with their
tails.   Seizing each other with their powerful jaws, the
stronger would dash about in the water, dragging the weaker
one with him, the jaws of the latter snapping impotently at
his foe.   The water was splashed high into the air and gradually became red with the blood from many frightful wounds.
We could do nothing but look on, except, indeed, to fill the
basin with water, so that the weaker animals might find refuge
underneath.

The next morning we allowed the water to run off and were then able to see the extent of the damage. All the warriors lay prostrate on the battlefield, every one of them shockingly mutilated and two of them quite dead. These two had had the whole of their under jaws and a great part of their upper jaws split in pieces. Of the other four, two had had their forelegs nearly torn off and hanging only by a shred of skin. The fifth had had its eye torn out, and the sixth had had the end of its tail bitten off. With the exception of the last they all died within a week, but he of the shortened tail slowly recovered and I was able subsequently to sell him.

After this incident I took careful precautions against any recurrence of these fights. Whenever a new alligator arrived I muzzled him by tying a cord tightly round his jaws before letting him out. This was rather a ticklish business, for when one had inserted one's hand in the box there were considerable odds that it might not come out again. When several animals which had arrived together were muzzled and turned out loose into a basin they would fall savagely upon one another, but could do each other no harm, and in about a week they would have quieted down sufficiently to make it safe to remove the muzzles. This I did by means of a knife fixed at the end of a long stick, which enabled me to cut the cord while standing at a safe distance. I then with a long hook pulled off the cords from the animal's snout. I never freed them all at the same time, but usually left several days before allowing all to enjoy their liberty. They had by that time become accustomed to one another, and no more fights of the kind above described occurred again.

After the alligators have been some little time in the basin and have become quite quiet, the question of feeding them arises. There is no hurry about taking any immediate steps, for these creatures, like snakes, can go without food for months together. The first food that I gave them consisted of the lungs of horses and cattle, which I cut into small pieces and threw into the water. I fed them only on the hottest days and usually in the evening. After they had learnt to know this method of feeding I was able to carry them on a step further. A large piece of meat was fixed to the end of a wooden pole and the water stirred about with it until the alligators seized it. I approached ever nearer the basin, and after from four to six weeks some of the animals had become so far tamed that they would take food from my hand. But I always felt that they would gladly have taken the hand as well if they had been given the chance. No real friendship can be established between these savage reptiles and human beings.

The smaller alligators, of three or four feet in length, which used to be kept in cages with glass fronts, can be tamed somewhat more quickly. It took me only about a week to teach these animals to come forward whenever I tapped on their glass windows, and take food out of my hand. The larger alligators are very voracious, and I have seen one nine feet long eat forty-eight pounds of meat at one meal.

Young alligators grow well in captivity if they are properly looked after. I should say that they reached their full development at the age of eighteen or twenty years. They are then about twelve feet long. I have never at any time seen one longer than this, though fourteen-feet specimens have been reported to have been shot. In the London Zoological Gardens a few years ago there was an animal eleven feet in length which had been bought eighteen years previously when only three feet long.

The animals referred to above belong to the species of alligator known as *Alligator mississippiensis*, coming from the Southern States of America. I well remember the first consignment of these which we ever received. This was in 1856. On hearing that the boat containing the animals had arrived, my father and I went on board to inspect them, and found there a miscellaneous collection of cages containing animals of all kinds. The owner demanded £120 for the whole collection, but we finally beat him down to £90 and carried away the lot. The dealer was so much pleased with this transaction that he made me a present of a young alligator three and a half feet long. It is true that it turned out to be blind in one eye, but it does not do to look a gift horse in the mouth, nor a gift alligator in the eye!

At this time alligators were very rare in Europe, and we made a very good business out of them. Even I, who was then only twelve years old, succeeded in selling my one-eyed alligator for eighteen shillings, which was to me a large fortune.

As compared with the great Indian crocodiles (or gavials) of the Ganges and the Brahmapootra, the American alligators are mere dwarfs. About fifteen years ago two skins of these crocodiles came into my possession, one fourteen and the other sixteen feet long. These I exhibited at Vienna, and they may still be seen in the Imperial Museum at that city. That they are not unusually large specimens, I have the evidence of my traveller Johansen, who states that three years ago, when navigating the Brahmapootra, he shot two gavials measuring fully twenty-five feet. He was, however, unable to secure their carcases, for the stream ran so strongly that it was impossible to stop the vessel. He says, moreover, that he has seen specimens of these animals quite thirty feet long; and now that he is again making a journey to India I have given him orders to bring home, if not the animal itself, at least some skins of it. I have several times tried to import the young of this species, but without success; they all died on the journey. I believe that these Ganges gavials are the largest crocodiles in existence, though my travellers have told me that those inhabiting the White Nile and the great African lakes reach enormous dimensions. Will it ever be possible to exhibit one of these gigantic creatures in captivity?

# CHAPTER VIII.

## ACCLIMATISATION AND BREEDING.

No fallacy is more widespread than that wild animals have to be kept throughout the winter carefully guarded from the effects of the low temperature. In Stellingen we keep lions, tigers, giraffes, ostriches, and other tropical animals wandering freely about in the open, though they always have access to cover if they should wish for it. The first thing that put this idea into my head was seeing a chimpanzee in England in a cold winter in the sixties disporting himself in the snow on the roof of a large tent. When he became cold he went in and took up a position by the stove. Later on I came across a menagerie in Westphalia where the monkeys were also allowed out of doors in the winter. Here there was an arrangement for connecting the outer enclosure with the inner cages by flaps, so that the creatures could pass at will from one to the other. The inner cages were kept at a temperature of 55° to 65° F., but the monkeys used to come out even when the thermometer was below zero.

It thus came about that very early in my career I pondered the question as to how far it was advisable to expose to our winter climate animals which came from tropical countries. The conclusion at which I arrived was attained by careful observation of the animals in my possession. My first experiment on the subject, however, was due to an accident rather than to any set purpose, and this occurred soon after I had been established at Neuer Pferdemarkt. I received one day in September a very beautiful Indian Cyrus crane. This we placed in an open enclosure where it remained until nearly the beginning of winter. About that time I was, as so often happens to me, called away unexpectedly and did not get back till about a week later. During this week cold weather suddenly set in. I arrived back very late at night, but was awakened early next morning by the characteristic cry of my crane, which I had forgotten all about, and which I had intended to transfer to a warm building. I hastened out to find the hoar frost lying on the ground, and expecting to see the crane frozen through with the cold. But to my astonishment I found him in the most boisterous health ; and when I came up, expecting to see him on the point of death, he came dancing and fluttering round to greet me, filling the air with his loud cries. Seeing that he did not appear to have suffered in any way from the cold, I arranged in one corner of the enclosure a sort of recess with plenty of straw where he could obtain shelter from the cold. But never once during the snowstorms, wind, and rain of that long winter did he make any use of this recess. He maintained his health in as perfect condition as though he were in his own tropical climate. I date from this occurrence the inauguration of my settled custom of giving wild animals access to the open air to the greatest possible extent. From this time commenced those experiments on acclimatisation which, since the founding of my animal park at Stellingen, have occupied a very large share of my attention.

The art of acclimatisation is as old as the animal trade itself, for it has always been necessary, in order to keep in captivity animals from foreign countries, to acclimatise them to some extent to their new country, as well as to changed habits of life and artificially prepared food. Captivity, indeed, involves an enormous change in all the animal's ordinary modes of life. From being free to roam on the deserts or the steppes, and compelled to exercise cunning or swiftness to secure its food, it is now confined in a comparatively cramped space and not called upon to exercise any of its normal activities whatever. The giraffes, elephants, and gazelles, which are accustomed to wander in large herds through the plains or forests, find themselves suddenly isolated and condemned to drag out their existence in solitary confinement. It is not to be wondered at that weakness and enervation should ensue as a result. Among all animals a sort of mental depression seems to take place when they have been only recently captured; and in the case of the more highly evolved and nervous animals, such as the anthropoids and especially the gorillas, this mental depression often terminates in death.

The power of adaptation to new climates varies greatly with different animals. It is most developed in the case of those animals which are accustomed to wander about on large continental plains, for there is there a considerable difference in the temperatures of day and night, and they are accustomed, in consequence, to suffer extremes. As long ago as the seventies I began acclimatisation experiments at Neuer Pferdemarkt with giraffes and elephants. One winter about that time was so severe that I was unable to raise the temperature of the stables in which the giraffes were kept to more than a few degrees above freezing-point, but I found that the cold did the creatures no harm. They grew a thick crop of winter hair, thus reacting to their new environment, and by the end of the winter their hair was about two and a half times as long as giraffe hair usually is.

In founding my animal park at Stellingen the chief principle which I kept in view was that each animal should be kept in an environment which differed as little as possible from its own natural environment. For this purpose one of the first requisites was to give them plenty of space to wander about in, so that their diminished freedom should be felt as little as possible. The next thing was to endeavour to harden them against the influence of the cold and wet, for which European climates are so remarkable. The case of African ostriches may be cited as a model of what can be done in this respect.

Ostriches in the snow.

Three years ago at the beginning of October there arrived at my animal park a number of young ostriches from Africa. Instead of being placed as usual in closed and heated buildings they were left out in a large yard in which a wooden hut had been set up as a shelter. During the whole winter the birds were kept in this yard and did very well, although the temperature several times reached 20° of frost. On the 1st January, 1906, when they were out at about 30° of frost, I noticed that some of them actually took the opportunity to give themselves baths in the snow. A cassowary, which was kept close by, likewise passed through the winter without harm. In 1907, six young ostriches about three and a half feet high arrived, and they also stood the winter very well. In the autumn we happened to receive half a dozen adult ostriches which had become so weak on the journey that they had to be carried out of their cages by their keepers. Nevertheless they were placed in the yard with the rest, and after a few hours in the open they had recovered sufficiently to be driven into the shelter hut with their comrades.

The hut is, of course, so arranged that the birds can go into it at any moment, should they be so inclined. For purposes of ventilation the windows of the hut are kept open day and night, so that there is little relief from the outer cold. The only furniture provided is a layer of turf and a plentiful supply of straw. Only for one week during the winter were the birds kept shut up in this hut, and that was simply on account of the ice on which they are so liable to slip that it brings them into great danger. During this period it is true that several accidents occurred. One ostrich had its leg broken while running about in the hut. Another died from the effects of a kick by one of its comrades. A third belied the common proverb about the digestion of ostriches. It swallowed eleven copper nails about one and a half inches long and also one of about four inches long, but instead of surviving and flourishing, as it ought to have done, it died through the nails piercing the wall of the stomach. But at no time did any accident occur on account of the severe weather. None of the creatures ever caught cold, and the six young ones, which in June weighed from 60 to 70 lbs. apiece, had by the following February reached an average weight of 340 lbs.

Successful acclimatisation experiments have been carried out with a variety of other animals besides ostriches. Remarkable results have been obtained with nearly all the different kinds of antelopes, with elands, gnus, beisas, etc.

Last winter we had, among other kinds, six specimens of

the Dorcas gazelle which gambolled about at a temperature several degrees below freezing-point just as cheerfully as if it had been summer. There is no doubt that all the species of antelope can be left out of doors throughout the winter so long as they have access to a covered shed where they can obtain shelter if necessary. When they are confined in close quarters they are much more liable to contract disease. The great antelope houses which most Zoo-

Dorcas gazelles in the snow.

logical Gardens possess are altogether a mistake, as also is the system of keeping the animals apart in separate stalls. They thrive much better when they are allowed to herd together, and any additional cost of tending or feeding the animals can be covered by breeding, for which the closer companionship naturally gives greater opportunities. In my garden, which has been specially laid out for the purpose of facilitating my acclimatisation experiments, I have hit upon several minor devices for giving shelter from rain and wind. The gables of the roofs project far out so as to afford shelter and a dry resting-place beneath, free from rain and snow. Some of the houses are so constructed that the outer door, instead of leading directly into the main building, opens into a passage which turns abruptly and so ex-cludes the possibility of draughts. The doors can then be left wide open day and night, summer and winter, nor is any artificial heating arrangement required. The animals obtain the benefit, however, of what I may call a natural heating

Lions in the snow.

arrangement. This is effected by allowing their dung to accumulate on the floor to the depth of about a foot. It is covered daily with fresh straw; but the warmth given out by the process of decomposition keeps the building at a tempera-ture considerably higher than that which prevails outside.

With the carnivores also, similar experiments have been undertaken; and they have been attended with similar

14

results.　Both lions and tigers, even Indian tigers, withstood the cold admirably so long as they were free to wander in the open.　It is true that I have at the back of my carnivore glen a shelter into which the animals can retreat at pleasure, and it is also true that this shelter was heated during some of the coldest days in the year.　But the heating was merely intended to keep it free from ice, and the animals were at all times at liberty to wander, and in fact did wander, outside, every day, even in the rain and snow.　One Indian panther which I had, became so much accustomed to the cold that it would not take advantage of the shelter, but lay out in the open all day on the branch of a tree.

The most remarkable case that I have observed of the beneficial effects of fresh air was in the case of two young lions which on their first arrival I kept confined within doors ; but here they fell into a pitiable condition and I thought they were going to die.　I then placed them out in the open, the only shelter provided being an ordinary box.　Forthwith they began to improve, and they are now perfectly recovered and have developed into fine animals.

Little has yet been done towards attempting the acclimatisation of monkeys, but I have now under construction several large monkey houses designed specially for this purpose.　In the case of the anthropoids, I have a couple of orangs already to a great extent acclimatised.　They had been kept in captivity in Borneo for six years before they reached me, and on their arrival I placed them in a large waggon cage, whence they have been in the habit of coming out daily and walking round the gardens with their keepers. Their health has remained uniformly good—a clear proof that creatures even from the tropical climate of Borneo can be acclimatised in this country.

There are, of course, many other animals that have been acclimatised besides those that I have mentioned.　In the winter my animal park shows scarcely less life and activity than in the summer.　Cyrus and crowned cranes, many exotic pheasants, and Australian black swans are all left out of doors throughout the entire winter. The marabou and the ibis can stand 10° of frost, and Australian cockatoos, aras, etc., do not have to take shelter even when the temperature sinks to 15° F. It is obvious, however, that there are many small tropical birds and mammals which it will never be possible to acclimatise. Reptiles and amphibians also are difficult subjects, though one never knows what may not be done until one has tried.

As I have already observed, the fundamental law of acclimatisation is to provide as large spaces as possible for the animals to roam about in. In Stellingen, moreover, I always try to supply an environment which resembles as far as possible the natural environment of the animals. I endeavour to consider the psychic as well as the physical condition of the animal, so that they should forget, if it be possible, that they are prisoners at all. The gregarious animals I always keep together in large enclosures. This goes a long way towards combating the tediousness which is one of the greatest difficulties to be overcome in keeping wild animals in captivity. Constant association enables them to play about together, keeps up the appetite, and maintains the body in a healthy condition. There are, therefore, in Stellingen wide tracts of meadow-land in which wander animals of many different species, though all are provided with shelters in case of unfavourable weather. Rocky ranges rise high into the air dotted with mountain animals from various parts of the world, and on a high plateau a herd of reindeer may be seen. A rock is provided, in as exact an imitation as possible of an iceberg, so that the polar bears may think that they are still in the Arctic regions; and there are great ponds with numerous. shelter corners in which seals, penguins, and water birds may feel that they are in their own home.

Certain other Zoological Gardens have been carrying out experiments of the same kind. In the acclimatisation of various exotic mammals and birds, Dr. Brandis in Halle has

achieved the best results, while Professor Heck of the Berlin
Zoological Gardens has been very successful in imitating the
natural surroundings of the animals.    At the Zoological Gardens at Copenhagen I was glad to find that many recom-
mendations which I had made five years previously had been
put into practice by Director Schiott with excellent results.    In
particular, the monkeys had been provided with an outer enclosure, to which they had access at all times.    Under this
treatment they had flourished so well that I endeavoured to
purchase some, but the director was not to be persuaded to
part with any.

One result of the acclimatisation of animals is that the erection of Zoological Gardens is no longer the expensive matter
that it used to be.    The massive houses with costly heating
arrangements can all be dispensed with, and there is no reason
at all why every town of 100,000 inhabitants should not have
its Zoological Gardens.    The planning required is both simple
and economical, and there would be little risk of loss.

Besides myself, various private persons in different parts of
the world have achieved considerable success in acclimatisation.    The famous Falz-Fein keeps all the animals on his
estate in the Crimea out in the open.    The Duke of Bedford
similarly keeps his fine collection roaming at large about the
great park at Woburn.    Mr. Walter Rothschild also has in
his parks very fine collections.    What greater pleasure can
there be to a private gentleman than that of maintaining and
establishing personal friendships with a large collection of
foreign animals!

I now have to touch upon one of the most serious problems with which the animal lover is confronted—I mean the
approaching extermination of many of the finest kinds of wild
beasts.    Antelopes, giraffes, and many other species become
scarcer year by year, and the difficulties of procuring
them are constantly increasing.    In order that they
may be saved, large reserves should without delay be established.    If it is not done soon, it will be too late.    The finest

Kangaroos in the snow.

country in the world for the establishment of such reserves would be Florida ; and, if any wealthy American could be persuaded to set aside even so small an area as 1,000 acres in that wonderful country, he would be performing a service, the importance of which can scarcely be exaggerated.   Giraffes, zebras, all the large species of antelopes, as well as the most beautiful cranes, ostriches, emus, etc., would live peaceably together in such a park.   Indeed it would almost be possible to transfer a complete portion of the African fauna to Florida if this were done.   The site selected for such a park would have to include woods and thickets, large meadows as well as hilly ground, and should be traversed by a river where the animals could go to drink.   If they were properly protected they would undoubtedly breed well and remain healthy.

There would be very little difficulty in carrying out this project.   If such a reserve on a small scale can be maintained in Southern Russia, where the temperature often falls many degrees below freezing-point, how much more easily could it be accomplished in the magnificent climate of the Southern States of America!   Nor would the expense be so very great ; $200,000 to $250,000 would be amply sufficient to cover the cost of all the animals that would be required.   Among the other animals that I have mentioned kangaroos could be easily included, for experience in my animal park has shown that they thrive admirably in such large spaces.

Closely connected with the subject of acclimatisation is the art of breeding, including the crossing of animals of different races.   This has always been one of the special points of interest in my garden at Stellingen.   It is very important from the commercial point of view on account of the prospect which it affords of improving some of our domestic races of animals.   From this standpoint careful attention ought to be paid to the indigenous cattle of uncivilised lands.   The acclimatisation of these is usually attended with but little difficulty, and a careful selection of them for breeding purposes might be attended with results very valuable to the farmer. We have at Stellingen done much business in importing Indian zebus for crossing purposes; and we export many of the animals to Argentina and Brazil. The draught capacity of cattle is very often immensely improved by the infusion of the zebu blood. The possibility of making such crosses is of the first importance in all the colonies, where a correct selection of suitable races of domestic animals is one of the most urgent problems that the people are called upon to solve.

FIG. 70.—Young argall.

I have already related the failure of my attempts at bringing home some of the giant wild sheep of Central Asia. It was suggested to me by Professor Kühn of Halle that I should endeavour to cross these with domestic sheep; but unfortunately the experiment has not yet proved practicable. I succeeded in bringing home some of the animals and also representatives of smaller races for the Royal Agricultural Institute, but it was only in the case of the smaller varieties that the crossing experiments were successful, for the giant sheep died very soon.

I do not despair, however, of succeeding ultimately in bringing home some of these giant wild sheep. I had the same difficulty at first with wild horses, stags, roes, ibexes, etc., but in all these cases experience showed me how I could overcome the obstacles and carry out the importation successfully. The Siberian stag crossed with the ordinary red deer gives very good results, and before long deer-stalkers may ex-

pect a great improvement in their stock from the result of such breeding. Falz-Fein was the first to produce this cross. Siberian roe-deer have also been crossed satisfactorily with our native roes.

The importation of Mongolian pheasants is also very profit-able for breeding purposes. My first orders for this bird were from the Duke of Bedford and from Mr. Walter Rothschild. The hybrids produced by crossing these pheasants with the ordinary English species are 30 per cent. heavier in weight than any which have hitherto been bred. The example of these two gentlemen has been followed by many others, especially in England, where pheasant shooting is a very popular pastime. I myself have gained little advantage from the importation of these birds, for they have to be brought from very distant and inaccessable countries at great expense and with many risks to be run by the way. If only 30 or 40 per cent. of the birds that are caught ultimately arrive at Hamburg I am fully satis-fied.

An interesting cross which has hitherto attracted little at-tention is that between the horse and the zebra. Professor Ewart of Edinburgh made some very successful experiments in this direction, and I bought from him all the hybrids which he obtained. Two of these "zebroids" were acquired by the British Government for use in the Mountain Artillery in India, and are said to have proved very satisfactory for this purpose. Two others, a stallion and a gelding, I have myself used for several years. They are excellent draught animals and as steadfast as ordinary mules. The latter, I may observe, deserve more attention than they receive in Germany. The Americans seem to understand the value of these hybrids better than we do, for according to some statistics which I saw some time ago, over a quarter of a million mules are bred in the United States every year.

# CHAPTER IX.

## ANIMALS IN SICKNESS.

In a collection consisting of thousands of animals, it is, of course, impossible to prevent the occurrence of various kinds of diseases. Sometimes these are very serious : as, for instance, when, just before the exhibition at Chicago, the epidemic of cholera invaded my menagerie and almost annihilated the inmates, while I and my skilled veterinary surgeons could do nothing but stand idly by and look on. But it is not often that we have to deal with scourges so terrible as this. Of the minor indispositions, those which affect animals on their first arrival, as a result of the long and trying journeys from the interior of distant continents and across the seas, are the most frequent. As I pointed out in the case of the elands and young baboons, their first acquaintance with captivity brings a heavy strain upon their constitutions, and the effects are very apt to appear later on in a disturbed state of health. Great care, therefore, has to be taken when one of these creatures arrives at its destination. It is fed on concentrated food in carefully regulated quantities. Every effort is made to soothe its disordered nerves, and to restore the creature to a normal condition before the process of acclimatisation is commenced. I lay great stress upon the rule that animals which have newly arrived should be treated very differently from those that have already been acclimatised and grown accustomed to their food. I feed new arrivals at frequent intervals during the day, giving them each time only small portions. Among the carnivores my rule is to feed them twice a day ; and not until they are thoroughly acclimatised can this rule be safely relaxed.

An adult lion when he has been acclimatised ought to receive from 13 to 17 lbs. of meat per day, with one fast day in the week. I usually give them alternately horse-flesh and beef ; and in the latter case I include both the head and the heart of the prey. This I do, not only from considerations of economy, but because I think it agrees well with the animals. Food which contains plenty of bone strengthens them and should always be given ; for there is no doubt of the truth of the proverb "bone makes bone". It is also very good for them to have to use their teeth. It preserves the teeth in a proper condition, and, by aiding the processes of mastication and digestion, gives the animals a cheerful temperament and keeps them in good health. It is quite astonishing what a large amount of bone a carnivore will succeed in devouring. Of the head of an ox or horse weighing 30 lbs. it will eat quite two-thirds. The strong bony feeding is also found to be beneficial in many illnesses, and when young animals are teething trainers like to feed them upon bony food in order to accelerate the development of the teeth. Even in adult animals I have found that a bone diet acts as a cure in cases of trouble with the teeth. I once had a fine specimen of a North African lion which suffered from severe fistula of the gums both around the canines and all along the upper jaw. In all such cases, where the disease can be diagnosed with comparative ease, I usually dispense with the services of a veterinary surgeon and attend to the matter myself. The first thing I did was to place the animal on a diet which would lead to no further inflammation of the sore parts. I gave him milk, eggs, and minced-up meat ; and the freedom from further irritation soon reduced the swelling of the gums and brought the animal into a more healthy condition. As soon as the inflammation had subsided I commenced to put him gradually on to a strong diet with a special liberality of bone. By thus compelling him to

use his teeth, the injured ones soon broke out of their own
accord, and it was unnecessary to resort to the operation of
removing them artificially—an operation always attended with
considerable danger on account of the use of anæsthetics which
it involves.

One of the most interesting cures which I have succeeded
in effecting was in the case of a small elephant which I
received on 9th March, 1904. He was at that time in a
very badly nourished condition, little more than skin and
bone, and on the point of collapsing. His height was only
four feet six inches at the shoulder. The care which I ex-

Strangling a sick elephant.

pended upon him was so well requited that in the course of
five weeks during July and August his weight increased from
nearly 7 cwt. to about 9½ cwt. Unfortunately he afterwards
contracted colic, which brought down his weight by about 1½
cwt within two days. He soon got over it, however, and
from the middle of September to the end of December put
on very nearly another 7 cwt. This remarkable cure was
effected without any resort to medicine. I may here take
the opportunity of observing that in dealing with wild animals
medicine should be avoided to the greatest possible extent.
I am wholly convinced that medicines often do more harm
than good ; and that the proper way of doctoring an animal

is to place it in such wholesome conditions that nature brings her own remedy without artificial assistance.

I had occasion not long ago to apply this doctrine in the case of a rhinoceros which had been wounded when it was being captured, and had been improperly treated while in transport. When it arrived it had in its back holes of the size of a man's hand, and a tendon of the hindleg was half cut through. The only medicinal treatment that I administered was to supply it with a hygienic bed—if that can be called medicinal. The bed in question is nothing more than dry earth covered over with hay or straw. I fed it on concentrated food such as eggs, milk, and water-gruel; and by the end of five weeks the rhinoceros had completely recovered its normal condition and looked strong and healthy.

One of the most remarkable cures that have been effected among the animals in my possession was in the case of an Indian buffalo-cow which had fallen ill before being shipped from India. The disease took the form of an inflammation on the snout and was accompanied by a heightened temperature and considerable pain, especially when the creature was feeding. An examination disclosed the fact that the abscess on the snout was crammed with parasitic worms. An attempt at a scientific cure, although it caused much suffering to the animal, was entirely unsuccessful, and after a time we had practically given up hope of being able to save its life. At this juncture an old Hindoo came upon the scene, and when we informed him of the various unsuccessful attempts to cure the buffalo he smiled knowingly and undertook to do the job himself in a single day. We attached little credence to the Hindoo's professions, but, since everything had failed and all hope been abandoned, there seemed no objection to letting him try what he could do. On receiving our permission, he went away and returned a few hours later with a bundle of blossoming branches of some shrub with which I was then, and am still, quite unacquainted. All I can say is that the blossom gave forth a somewhat

penetrating odour. We imagined that the Hindoo was about
to make a decoction from these plants to wash out the sores
—but no such thing. He merely tied the branches securely to
the buffalo's tail. This so irritated the animal that it lashed
its tail about, hitting itself over the snout in its endeavours
to tear off the branches. The constant contact of the snout
with the shrub very quickly produced a remarkable effect. I
cannot say whether the worms in the abscess were stupefied by
the odour, or whether they merely disliked it and endeavoured
to escape from it. But certain it is, that without further
trouble they all fell out of their own accord, so that we were
immediately able to wash out the abscess, and the creature
was soon completely healed. This affords an interesting
illustration of the variety of experience which I have collected
in the course of my business.

Although this method of healing seems pretty simple, it is
not more simple than many of the methods which I regularly
adopt. Except in cases of infectious diseases, I have all my
life confined myself to old-established and well-known
remedies. I rarely call in a veterinary surgeon, and, indeed,
it would be impracticable for me to do so whenever any of
my thousands of animals happens to get a cold in the head
or a pain in the toe. Common-sense is the most necessary
qualification for dealing with these minor ailments. A
careful examination has to be made of the sick animal, and
then one has to take the best means available for getting
it right again.

As an instance of my method of procedure in such matters,
I may recount the story of a polar bear which I purchased
about forty years ago from the Zoological Garden at Copenhagen. He was an unusually fine and large specimen and
had been there several years, being probably about twelve
years old. Owing, however, to the inadequate arrangements
of the space allotted to him he was suffering from a complaint
which is very common among polar bears. If any one will
watch these creatures in a Zoological Garden he will observe

that, when they turn round, they twist round shortly on their hind-quarters. In these turns and in all their other movements the hind-paws are scarcely moved at all, so that the claws growing upon them have nothing to keep them short and grow to an immoderate length, while those on the fore-paws are worn out with constant use. The hind-claws thus grow right into the flesh, and, in the case above alluded to, they had not only grown into the flesh, but gone right through it and come out on the other side. When I bought this bear, the authorities at the Zoological Garden at Copenhagen had given up hope of being able to cure it; but after considerable thought I determined to attempt the following experiment. I had a large transport cage built about four feet six inches high and seven feet long and only one foot six inches wide. The front of the cage consisted simply of a grating made of parallel bars. Into this cage I drove the bear from out of his ordinary den. My purpose was to get at his hind-paws without either putting him under anæsthetics or tying him down ; so, when once he was in the cage, I secured the services of the two assistants, who were all I then possessed, and tilted the cage over until the grating was at the bottom with the bear standing upon it. We next hoisted up the cage, which, with the bear in it, was not far short of half a ton, and rested it upon strong blocks, leaving room, however, for me to crawl underneath it. When I did this I could without difficulty tie down the bear's paw to the grating, and it was then a very simple matter to cut the long claws with a pair of strong clippers. I pulled out the stumps of the claws from the inflamed and mortified flesh, and hoped that after this operation he would soon become healthy again. In this hope I was completely justified. I transferred him immediately to another small cage, the lower half of which was lined with zinc, and, as soon as I had got him into this, I filled the lined portion of the cage with ice-cold water. The creature was thus kept continuously with his hind-paws immersed in the cold water. I kept a constant stream running, so that it was always clear and fresh, and I devised means for keeping it thoroughly cool at the same time. In a fortnight the cure had entirely succeeded, and the bear once more became an almost perfect specimen of his kind. Some time after, I sold him to a menagerie for a very good price.

Every one who has had anything to do with animals is well acquainted with the fact that they often have a strong predilection for alcohol and sugar. Thus it is well known that race-horses are given sack to drink, or have their nostrils washed out with it, before they start in a race. Monkeys, too, are fond of wine, or of alcohol in any other form. Once when I was transporting seven elephants and a number of other animals through Germany the elephants were seized with colic. In order to cure them of this I gave them doses of rum. One of them, however, appeared to have had rather too much, for he became exceedingly hilarious and challenged his more sober neighbour to a duel. The jovial monster was disturbing the entire menagerie, so I saw that there was nothing for it but to repeat the dose, for the purpose of reversing the effect. I therefore supplied him with a large extra quantity of grog. He then became completely drunk, and soon fell into a quiet sleep.

I have heard of a case of alcohol being administered also to bears in a very cruel, indeed a revolting, manner. This occurred some time ago when I had sold several large European bears to a menagerie owner of the name of Malferteiner. This man used to wander about the country with an itinerant exhibition, and his cages were of a somewhat light make, scarcely strong enough to keep securely the exceptionally fine animals which I had sold him. There seemed considerable danger that, by gnawing, scratching, or breaking, they would soon succeed in gaining their liberty. He was therefore rather pleased when, soon afterwards, he fell in with a tribe of gypsies, who were much interested in the bears and offered to purchase them. As they had some ready money he completed the transaction; and waited with curiosity to see how the gypsies were going to take over the captives, for they had no luggage and no cages in which they could keep the bears. When Malferteiner asked them how they were going to manage it, they replied that he need not worry about that, they would look after it. He could not see, however, how they were going to avoid running into considerable danger; for no attempt had ever been made to tame the bears or break them in in any way. The first thing that the gypsies did was to leave the creatures for a couple of days without food. They then brought a cask of salted herrings, which they put in the cages. The bears did not like this food at all, but their dislike availed them nothing, for no other was offered them; and on the third day their hunger became so acute that they devoured the herrings. Forthwith they became, of course, exceedingly thirsty, but no water was given them. Instead of water, bowls of sweetened spirit were placed before them, and this they greedily lapped up. They were then thoroughly intoxicated and sank into a very deep sleep. The gypsies were now in a position to carry out their evil purpose without fear. They walked into the cages where the formidable animals lay as harmless and motionless as sacks of flour; they extracted their large canine teeth with pliers, and cut away the claws from their paws. Even the deep wounds in the flesh which they made in this operation did not arouse the bears, and the gypsies knew no pity. Rings were drawn through their noses, and to each animal two chains were attached, one round the neck and another to the ring in the nose. The creatures had now been altogether deprived of their weapons of offence and defence. They were placed upon a cart, and the gypsies drove off with them. After many hours the unfortunate animals awoke and fell out of the cart; but, held as they were by the chains, they were compelled to run behind. The gypsies had taken the additional precaution of muzzling them, but this was entirely unnecessary, for the poor brutes, stupefied and weakened by pain, had no spirit left for attacking

15 *

their persecutors. Let us hope that in these civilised days such barbarous and cruel treatment would be impossible. Under enlightened laws the punishment would indeed be swift and severe for offenders of this detestable description.

One of the most remarkable diseases which afflict animals in captivity takes the form of the infliction by the creatures themselves of dangerous wounds upon their own bodies. This peculiar complaint only occurs among the carnivores, but it is liable to break out in any species belonging to that order. I have had two cases of this self-mutilation in the case of spotted hyænas, which up to that moment had appeared to be in thoroughly good health and very well behaved. In both cases these creatures all of a sudden broke forth into loud yells and literally fell upon themselves, tearing great pieces out of their own bodies. So quickly and so unexpectedly did this happen that there was no time to do anything to save them, and in each case the wounds inflicted were so shocking that the animals soon expired. Some years ago also a large jaguar became afflicted in the same way. He attacked one of his own paws, and so severely did he injure it that he had to be kept on a sick bed for four months and was not completely recovered for six months. Although I have never known male lions to be taken in this way, I have on two separate occasions observed it in lionesses. These two animals both ate their own tails as far as they could reach, and as a result so much blood was lost that they both had to be killed. A tiger in my possession once did the same thing. He ate away half his tail, and it was only with great care and difficulty that we succeeded in healing him. Although I have watched with great care, I have not succeeded in finding any cause for these horrible habits. All the animals which I have here mentioned had been up to the moment of their seizure in thoroughly good health. They had not refused to take their food, nor betrayed any other symptom of approaching illness. The common reason given for these attacks is that the animal is suddenly possessed with an inordinate desire for blood, but it seems to me much more probable that it is due to some disease of the brain. Whatever may be its cause, it is certainly of the greatest interest; and it is much to be wished that some authoritative man of science would undertake a research into its origin.

# CHAPTER X.

## LIFE AT STELLINGEN.

I HAVE already described the process whereby, in the course of a few years, wide flat plains, fit for nothing but potato fields, and uncultivated land, interspersed by a few bushes, have been converted into a magnificent park. It is true that the hills and dales of this area do not accord well with the flat expanse of Northern Germany, but they are admirably suited to the purpose for which they were created. Under the precipitous cliffs and through the green meadows run small rivulets, spanned here and there by bridges so as to give a very picturesque effect.

In each portion of this animal park there are kept the kinds of animals most suited to that special part; so that, within the limits of the park itself, there are contained specimens representing the fauna of every part of the globe. The stranger should direct his steps towards the group of buildings in the centre of the park; for when he stands there and looks outwards, he can obtain a fine view over every part of this veritable animal paradise.

In the foreground is a large lake for the water birds, on which may be seen many varieties of swans, geese, and ducks. Beyond this there rises a rocky cliff, and on either side of it there stretch wide meadows, in which may be seen flamingoes, cranes, pelicans, and ibises disporting themselves in the sun. This great expanse of lowland stretches far away to the foot of those rocky hills seen in the distance, and across the plain there roam so many different kinds of herbivores that one might fancy oneself in the Garden of Eden. Sheep,

Wa er-birds a Stellingen.

goats, and antelopes stand out prominently on the hillsides ; whilst below in the green valley may be seen brahma-zebus from India, grazing side by side with shaggy yaks from Mongolia, guanacoes from South America, and woolly lamas from Peru. Here also is to be found the great dromedary and the conspicuously marked zebra. Various kinds of deer which have come from distant lands mingle with their German congeners. Mighty buffaloes and tiny dwarf goats graze peaceably together ; and although all is peace and harmony, the scene presented is one of incessant movement, the animals appearing to enjoy complete liberty.

As one looks beyond this large prairie the spectacle presented becomes still more remarkable ; for, only a few steps from where the herbivores are enclosed, a number of lions may be observed wandering about in a rocky gorge, not shut in by any fence ; while beyond these again a high mountain fills the horizon, on which may be seen all manner of Alpine creatures. Outlined against the sky beyond a markhor-buck stands on a lofty ridge ; and, even as we watch, it gallops off and takes a flying leap over a deep chasm lying in its path. Just as on the plain below many different animals are collected together, so also

Flamingoes.

on this rocky mountain. Maned sheep from North Africa, the famous wild sheep of Siberia, large families of Himalayan wild goats and many other species find here plenty of scope for the exercise of their rock-climbing proclivities.

The liberty which is accorded to the animals, and which goes so far to relieve the distress that a life in captivity must mean, is not only apparent but real. In the case of the lions in particular there is amply sufficient space for them to exercise

their powerful muscles; and visitors as a rule cannot conceive at first what barrier there is to keep them in. The
broad trench which serves this purpose is so carefully con-
cealed with thick brushwood and plants that the illusion is
almost complete.

It is only in comparatively recent years that I have
ventured to exhibit animals in this fashion. The first occasion was at the Berlin Exhibition in 1896, and later on I
tried it at Leipsic and several other places, but my greatest

The " Japanese " Island.

success was at the St. Louis Exhibition in 1904. Before
substituting a trench for railings, I had, of course, to carry
out a series of experiments to discover how far the animals
could jump. Any underestimate of their saltatory powers
might, indeed, be attended with terrible consequences. I
therefore investigated carefully their capacity both at the high
jump and the long jump. In the case of the feline carnivores
my experiments were made some time ago when I was still
at Neuer Pferdemarkt. For the high jump my method was
to take a stuffed pigeon and fix it to a projecting branch of a

tree about ten feet above the ground.    I then let loose in turn lions, tigers, and panthers into the enclosure where the tree was growing, and, as soon as they spied the pigeon, they exerted themselves to the utmost to bring it to the ground.    They were, however, unable to do so.    The lions and tigers could only jump about six feet six inches.    The panthers were more athletic and could just reach the branch, but even they were unable to bring down the pigeon, for the latter was fixed to the highest point.

The long jump I used to test in a similar manner, using for the most part animals which had already received some training and were therefore more adept than ordinary unpractised carnivores.    The panthers could just cover ten feet without a run ; but, if they had been able to take a run, I feel sure that they could have increased it to thirteen or fourteen feet.    Tigers I found could also just cover ten feet from a standstill, but I doubt not that they also could have put on several feet if they had been allowed a run.

On the strength of these experiments I considered it safe to surround the carnivore gorge at Stellingen with a trench twenty-eight feet wide.    Although they could easily take a ten-yard run at it, it is certain that, if they endeavoured to leap so wide a chasm, they would inevitably fall into the depths of the abyss.    I had, however, to devise an arrangement to safeguard the animals from falling into the trench inadvertently while playing about.    For this purpose I caused to be constructed a ledge some five feet wide, running round the trench on the inner side a little distance below the top. It is true that this somewhat diminished the distance from the outer side of the trench ; but it has to be remembered that an animal taking off from this ledge would not have the advantage of a run, and would therefore find in it no facility for getting out.    When thus confined by a trench, the animals are indeed much more securely locked up than if they were kept behind bars.    For bars may be, and often have been, broken through, but it is a physical impossibility that the animals should take so wide a leap as that which would be necessary to escape.

The large park constitutes a community resembling in many ways a community of human beings. The passing visitor has but little idea of the varying incidents and occupations which fill the lives of the captive animals. As in a community of human beings, they make friends and enemies among one another; they fall in love, and fall out of it again. There are births, deaths, and marriages, and a constant supply of news for the men whose duty it is to look after the creatures. Indeed there would be sufficient material to fill the columns of a small daily newspaper. Careful observation is constantly kept on all the animals, and treatment is meted out to each according to its individual requirements.

Here, for instance, is a piece of news which comes in one morning from the Arctic Panorama, the rocks and waters of which are inhabited by polar bears, by reindeer, by various aquatic birds, and by walruses and other pinnipeds. The news is not, perhaps, of fundamental importance; yet it is interesting in our little township. One of the seals, known as a sea-bear (a species of pinniped, by the way, which has never before been seen in Europe), has discovered a new way of amusing himself. His plan is to conceal himself beneath the surface of the water, and there narrowly observe the sparrows fluttering about on the brink. Then he would suddenly with lightning speed flash out of the water and seize a sparrow, with which he would slide back gently into the pond. There he would callously drown it, and, when it was no longer able to fly away, he would play about with it for an hour or more. This animal was much given to sport of this kind, and a few days later he succeeded in catching a rat which he maltreated after the same fashion.

In the case of this sea-bear it was, of course, the love of play and not mere wanton cruelty which caused it to worry the sparrow and the rat. Love of play is, indeed, strongly developed in all animals, and contrivances should be invented

In the Arctic Panorama.

Sea-lions an

to give them every opportunity of indulging the faculty. I have already at Stellingen séveral contrivances of this kind, and intend shortly to introduce a great many more. To each creature should be given whatever seems to suit him best. Sea-lions, for instance, have a natural talent for balancing; and they will derive much amusement from so simple a thing as a rod thrown into the water. The rhinoceros, on the other hand, is not qualified for performances in which delicacy and precision are required. Brute strength is his forte, and some means must be devised for providing him with an opportunity to exercise it. In the stable of one of our rhinoceroses, called Max, we have tried a contrivance which has proved very successful. A long pole has been inserted horizontally across the stable at a considerable height from the ground; and from it is suspended a heavy sack of hay somewhat resembling on a large scale those appliances upon which American boxers are wont to exercise themselves. Max at once took to the idea of this sport. He commenced boxing furiously with the sack, and has never since become bored with the pastime. For wild cattle, too, which are more cut out for feats of strength than for anything requiring subtlety or precision, we provide a barrel which they can roll to and fro or send hurtling into the air with their horns. "Panem et Circenses" is the motto to be observed, if the population is to be kept in a wholesome frame of mind.

Besides feeding and amusements, there is another factor of great importance in the lives of the animals, *viz.*, the loves and friendships which they form among one another. If they could talk, what endless gossip there would be in our little community! It would doubtless turn to a great extent upon the *mésalliances* which take place. For among beasts, as among men, *mésalliances* frequently occur. What can be more grotesque, what can form a more appropriate subject for gossip, than an affection between a great cow-elephant and a male kangaroo? Yet this actually did take place. Every day the two animals would play together, the elephant caress-

16

ing the marsupial with her trunk; and they hated to be separated from one another. Other cases I have already referred to in preceding chapters: as when a male elephant made friends with a little pony mare, or when a crowned crane became intimately associated with an American ostrich. I also had an instance of friendship between a drake and a gull. The life has its shady side too, for there is no end of jealousy accompanying the various demonstrations of affection.

Among the most interesting inhabitants of the park are the walruses, who live in the Arctic Panorama. Arctic

Walruses.

travellers are unanimous in recording that these animals in a wild state are very unpleasant to meet, and occasionally extremely pugnacious. If they are irritated, they will often attack a boat and endeavour to capsize it with their mighty tusks. For modern sportsmen, armed with weapons of

unfailing accuracy, the walrus has, however, lost most of his terrors. His powerful weapons of defence avail him little. Even the primitive Eskimos succeed in slaying these aquatic monsters. They first harpoon them, and then, as soon as they can come to close quarters, attack them mercilessly with lances, the animals soon succumbing from the countless wounds inflicted upon them. The walrus has very rarely been exhibited in captivity; and I may therefore consider myself fortunate in that I have received during recent years several separate consignments of the creatures. Of course, it is only possible to capture them alive when they are quite young. I understand that mine were secured by surprising them on the ice and seizing them after their parents had been slain.

The first two walruses which I received both died within a few weeks; two others which I had later on lived for nearly two years. They are very sensitive, and require careful looking after, being especially liable to catch cold. The last of these first four walruses caught a cold when winter was coming on, but we succeeded in curing the animal by the agency of a steam bath. It lived till it was about three years old, and, when it died, it weighed fully 8 cwt. I believe that a walrus is full-grown at about ten years of age, and it then weighs about a ton and a quarter. I need hardly say that such large animals require a prodigious quantity of food. To the first two which I had, in spite of their youth, I gave over 20 lbs. a day. Cod, halibut, and various kinds of fish were the staple food. I cut it up into small pieces, and took out the bone, so that the animals could easily consume the pieces in the water. The second two walruses that I received used to devour between them no less than 180 lbs. of fish daily, though they were at that time not three years old. From this it may easily be inferred how great must be the appetite of a full-grown walrus and how prodigious the quantity of food which he has to catch.

It was only after much trouble and many disappointments that I succeeded, in October, 1907, in obtaining more walruses for my garden. In that month, however, I secured three individuals which had been captured in the Kara Straits near Waigatz Island, and were sent me by Dr. Breitfuss, the leader of a scientific expedition to those parts. Their captor fed them exclusively on the blubber of the common seal, and when they first arrived at Stellingen the same diet was continued. But, after a time, all the available blubber came to

16 *

an end, and it became necessary to give the animals some
other food. I therefore offered them codfish, but this, although
it was readily accepted by the two females, was persistently
refused by the male. I thought I should see him perish of
starvation before my very eyes, until I tried the experiment
of offering him some shark. This he devoured with seeming
satisfaction, thus breaking a fast of no less than a fortnight.
Later on he consented to eat codfish like the females, but the
bones always had to be carefully extracted before it was given
to him. Feeding walruses is in fact rather like feeding children. The food is held out invitingly before them and they
take it piece by piece. But their appetites are very far from
childish. Last month the three young walruses devoured no
less than 2½ tons of fish costing me over £30.

In September, 1908, my collection was enriched by the
addition of five more walrus cubs, two males and three females.
Thus I am now able to exhibit eight of these animals—a fact
of which I think I am justified in being proud, seeing that
there are none in any other Zoological Garden in the world,
except that at Copenhagen, and there only one. These five
were brought me from Hammerfest by a certain Captain
Hansen, who gave me much interesting information about
their habits in the wild state, as well as about the mode of
catching them. Captain Hansen, who is a Norwegian by
birth, has had considerable experience of hunting walruses,
which he has carried on in the Arctic Seas ever since 1886.
For the last sixteen years he has been captain of a ship of his
own which he calls *The Seventh of June* after the date of his
own baptism.

The walruses are killed by harpooning; and for this
purpose a peculiar kind of boat is built, about twenty feet
long and seven feet wide. The boat is not clinker-built like
ordinary boats, for the planks of which it is made, instead
of overlapping, fit exactly into one another, leaving the
outer surface of the boat quite smooth. The floor of the
boat is lined with metal, and there is in the forepart a

platform carrying an upright post firmly fixed at the bottom. To this post is attached the end of the very long line fastened to the harpoon. When a walrus is to be har-pooned, a man stands upon the platform, with the line lying loosely upon it ready for use. After the animal has been harpooned, the line is drawn through a notch at the side of the boat, for it would, of course, be very dangerous if the walrus, in swimming backwards and forwards, were able to pull the line freely over the boat. Eight of these notches are provided, as it often takes several harpoons to kill one walrus. A boat's crew consists of four men, of whom three row, while the fourth stands on the platform and hurls the harpoon. The distance at which it is usually thrown is about twenty-five yards; and I am told that the record is thirty-seven yards. As soon as it is harpooned the walrus dives, and the harpooner knows by the slackening or tightening of the line whether the animal is coming towards him or going in the opposite direction. In the latter case, which usually happens when females have been struck, there is not much danger; but in the former case the crew have to be very sharply on the look-out, for the wounded animal will rise quite close to the boat and attempt to attack his enemies. But even when the line becomes taut and the creature swims rapidly away, the line often has to be cut to avoid being capsized. This is especially frequent when the harpooned walrus has been lying on an ice-floe, and makes for the water on the opposite side of the floe from the boat. Similarly, when a walrus herd has been surprised whilst lying on the coast, it is usual first to kill the animals nearest the water, in order to block the way of escape for those which happened to be farther inland. When they have been harpooned the walruses are despatched as quickly as possible with guns, especially constructed by the Nor-wegians for the purpose. The capture of some of my last walruses nearly cost the hunters their lives; for the young cubs which had been brought on board gave out such appealing cries for help, that a gigantic male was attracted and delivered a furious attack upon the boat, driving three great holes through it with his tusks.

The commonest way of catching young walruses is to kill the mother ; indeed this is usually necessary before the capture can be carried out. One of the animals I now have at Stellingen was caught in a very ingenious though pathetic manner. The mother was first killed and drawn into close proximity with the boat, which was then allowed to remain still. Before very long the cub came looking for his mother, and having found her, climbed up on her back, where he was easily caught and secured. On the voyage when the hunters captured the five walruses which I have mentioned as being recently added to my collection, no fewer than sixty-eight others were killed. The captors were able to sell their hides for £3 19s. per cwt. Captain Hansen says that the largest walruses are to be found in Franz-Josef Land. During last year's catch an animal was found there with tusks two feet six inches long and weighing 5½ lbs. each. They were sold for about 3s. 2d. per lb.

Except during the pairing season, in September and October, the sexes among the walruses live separately, the young going about with the females. Thus in the year 1886 Captain Hansen found on the north coast of North-East Land a herd of 370 individuals, all females. Every one of them was slaughtered by five ships' crews. The females also frequent the north coast of Spitzbergen at about 81° N. latitude. The males, on the other hand, may be found in Storefiord, the straits between Spitzbergen and Edge Island. The largest male seen by the hunters on their last voyage weighed nearly 3 tons. This animal they were fortunate enough to kill, and its hide alone weighed nearly half a ton. The young were caught near Cape Flora in Northbrook Island, but the richest hunting-ground is now the north coast of Siberia.

According to Captain Hansen, the food of walruses consists mainly of minute marine animals, which swim or float near the surface of the ocean, and in particular they consume a large number of tiny crustaceans. In addition to these they devour a large number of sand-worms, which are found in great quantities in the stomachs of the captured animals. On one occasion Hansen saw a walrus attacking a dead seal. He had already made large holes with his tusks in the carcase and was sucking away at the blubber. Unfortunately Hansen was unable to ascertain whether the walrus had killed the seal, or merely found it dead.

The tusks of the females are about one-third shorter than those of the males, and are also thinner and not so heavy.

Walruses roar with such a terrific sound that it can be heard for two and a half miles down wind; indeed so penetrating is it, that, when there are fogs, the hunters often lay their ship's course by the sound of the roaring.

The danger of hunting these animals may be illustrated by the following incident. In the year 1897, near King Charles Land, in the course of a walrus hunt, a careless harpooner omitted to place the line in its notch, foolishly leaving it loose on the side of the boat, after he had speared a walrus. His carelessness resulted in the boat being capsized, and all its four occupants killed. It happened that the animal which they had attacked was a powerful male who immediately made for his antagonists. The first one he came to he instantly pierced through the back with both tusks. Four times did he come to the surface of the water, and each time he picked off one of the four men until they had all been annihilated. Two of them endeavoured to escape by swimming away, but the infuriated animal speedily overtook them. The fourth clambered on to the top of the overturned boat, but that availed him nothing. The walrus attacked the boat with such violence that the man was unable to keep his hold, and shortly fell a victim to the animal's fierce vengeance.

I was extremely interested to watch the behaviour of my

three older walruses when the five new arrivals were first introduced to them at Stellingen. These five were brought along to their new home in cages placed in a cart. Before ever the cart arrived in sight of the old walruses, the latter appeared to know that some of their kind were near at hand. Whether they smelt them or heard them I cannot say ; but the fact remains that they

Penguin.

fell into a state of extraordinary excitement. The male came out of the water, followed by the two females, and they all three set up a terrific bellowing. It was curious to note how they foamed at the mouth and how their eyes became bloodshot with excitement. When the young ones were released from their cages the older residents received them with every sign of a warm welcome, coming up all round them and sniffing at them. Indeed the high intelligence and sense of fellowship which has been supposed to characterise these animals was fully borne out on the present occasion. I called to the keeper to bring some fish and we then straightway commenced to feed the creatures.

Feeding walruses when they are first caught is not a very easy matter. I am told that in the case of the last consignment, the first two cubs to be captured refused to eat for nine days. The third, however, only fasted for two days, and it was through his good example that the others also commenced to eat. When the whole party arrived at Stellingen there was no difficulty, for they quickly perceived the anxiety of the older walruses to secure the food, and proceeded to emulate their example with the most vigorous appetites. Before long they were as tame and confiding as if they had been in the park all their lives.

I may now give some statistics as to the population of my animal community and their necessaries of life. In August, 1908, I took a census of all my animals, which worked out as follows :—

15 orangs, chimpanzees and gibbons.

109 monkeys of 22 different species.

91 feline carnivores, including 49 lions, 26 tigers, and 3 lion-tiger hybrids.

18 polar bears.

12 bears of other species.

40 hyænas and canine carnivores of 15 different species.

13 elephants.

3 hippopotami.

2 African rhinoceroses.

4 tapirs.

3 giraffes.

21 camels, dromedaries, and lamas.

57 deer.

43 head of cattle, including 12 bison and 17 buffalo.

84 wild sheep, domestic sheep, ibexes, and goats, of 18 different species.

43 antelopes, including elands, water-bucks, kudus, etc.

1 wart-hog.

73 equine herbivores, including 21 zebras.

In the Arctic Panorama :—

3 walruses.

4 sea-lions.

1 sea-bear.

3 smaller seals of different species.

96 rodents of 8 different species.

8 armadillos.

12 kangaroos.

There were 1,072 birds, including 48 African ostriches, 18 South American ostriches, 11 Australian ostriches, 13 cassowaries, 295 swimming birds, 273 waders, of which 90 were flamingoes and 82 cranes, 16 birds of prey, 187 fowls, 116 song birds, 69 parrots, and 21 toucans.

Among reptiles I had 36 turtles, 11 crocodiles and alligators, and 68 snakes.

The community consisted, therefore, of nearly 2,000 inhabitants, worth over £50,000.

It may easily be imaginèd that the commissariat of this community is no easy matter to manage. A full-grown lion or tiger consumes every day from 10 to 15 lbs. of meat, while an elephant, even when not working, receives 10 lbs. of oats, 5 lbs. of bran, 40 lbs. of rapes and 60 lbs. of hay—an allowance which has to be increased when it is made to do work. A hippopotamus cannot do with less than 10 lb. of crushed oats, 6 lb. of bran, 16 lb. of rye bread, 20 lb. of rapes, and 20 lb. of hay per diem. The animals are not accustomed to dainties ; yet from the following list may be seen the great variety of food which they receive. The list is taken from the records of the kitchen department, showing the amount consumed in one year :—

| | | | | | |
|---|---|---|---|---|---|
| 85,980 kilogms.[1] of horseflesh. | | | 6,350 kilogms. of cabbage. | | |
| 26,093 | ,, | beef. | 250 | ,, | lettuce. |
| 84 score pigeons. | | | 200 | ,, | John's bread. |
| 250 | ,, | rabbits. | 800 | ,, | oil cake. |
| 120 | ,, | fowls. | 3,500 | ,, | acorns and |
| 48,184 kilogms. of fish. | | | | | chestnuts. |
| 9,602 | ,, | white bread. | 300 | ,, | dates. |
| 14,931 | ,, | rye bread. | 1,200 | ,, | bananas. |
| 8,342 | ,, | horse cakes. | 5,200 score eggs. | | |
| 6,360 | ,, | dog biscuits. | 19,039 litres[2] of milk. | | |
| 15,800 | ,, | maize. | 1,380 kilogms. of oatmeal. | | |
| 16,200 | ,, | crushed maize. | 43,260 | ,, | straw. |
| 9,600 | ,, | wheat. | 89,249 | ,, | hay. |
| 28,130 | ,, | oats. | 150,600 | ,, | Timothy hay. |
| 44,684 | ,, | crushed oats. | 15,900 | ,, | clover. |
| 11,886 | ,, | maslin. | 1,100 | ,, | hemp. |
| 5,200 | ,, | barley. | 1,300 | ,, | buck wheat. |
| 46,000 | ,, | bran. | 850 | ,, | millet. |
| 900 | ,, | peas. | 3,300 | ,, | rice. |
| 5,500 | ,, | potatoes. | 7,500 | ,, | alpine hay and |
| 900 | ,, | horse molasses. | | | reindeer moss. |
| 5,920 | ,, | carrots. | 105,000 | ,, | grass. |
| 120,000 | ,, | rapes. | 6,450 | ,, | chopped straw. |

[1] There are slightly more than 1,000 kilogrammes to a ton.
[2] There are about 1¾ pints to a litre.

To this list I should add meat soups, milk and fruit soups, whortleberry wine, meal, cherries, grapes, and other fruits for the apes; further, nearly 50,000 kilos of rye and oat straw, as also (though it hardly comes into this reckoning) 20,000 kilos turf-litter for the beds, and about 200,000 kilos coke and charcoal. The cost of all this amounts, in round figures, to £7,500.

The animal park is far from being yet completed. Only this year a second portion of it was opened, in which the ethnographic exhibitions are to be held and which is to contain a new performing theatre. In the coming year a third

Newly-arrived penguins being fed.

large portion is to be opened, including a miniature railway running round a pond. On the banks of the pond there will be scattered artistic life-size representations of various prehistoric animals, so that the visitor may fancy that he has been transported back thousands of centuries in time. The ceratosaurus, fifty feet high, and the stegosaurus will both be there;

while among the tree-tops the thunder-lizard, the monstrous brontosaurus of one hundred and fifty feet long, will raise its head. The remaining part is to contain an ape house, a large monkey house, the ostrich farm, and other enclosures.

Besides these various undertakings, I have recently purchased a new piece of ground to the north-east of the present portion of my park. Here another farm is being made, where new experiments in breeding cattle and equine animals are to be carried out. These experiments have already begun, but it will take several years before the arrangements are complete. Money is the first necessity for the execution of these projects, and I have therefore to exercise careful supervision in order to ensure that the business should be economically conducted.

Let me take this opportunity of correcting an erroneous impression which has received widespread currency. It is not the case that any Bank or Financial Syndicate has any interest in the multifarious business situated at Stellingen. Both the park and the business itself are my own private property. The neighbouring land, on the other hand, belongs, as I have already explained, to a limited Company in which I possess a certain interest.

# CHAPTER XI.[1]

## THE OSTRICH-FARM AT STELLINGEN.

Not very long ago it would have been considered a wild dream if anybody had suggested that it were possible in the latitude of Hamburg to allow ostriches out of doors in the winter ; and it would have appeared still more incredible that an ostrich-farm should be established in that locality. Yet this has now become a *fait accompli.* Since the early months of 1909, when the ostrich-farm at Stellingen was first inaugurated, the many doubters have been convinced of its practical success. While this marks an era in the progress of the art of managing wild animals, it holds out at the same time promise of a valuable trade in ostrich feathers.

The idea of attempting to acclimatise ostriches did not occur to me all of a sudden. During the first three winters of the present century, when I used to keep ostriches in the ordinary manner in heated stables, I lost no fewer than twenty of these birds. I thought that their death might be attributable to the fact of their confinement in close stables, without opportunity for movement ; and I determined to test the accuracy of this opinion by an experiment. So in the winter of 1903-4 I allowed my African ostriches, as also a two-spotted cassowary, to have access to the open air—except when there was slippery ice which would make it dangerous. All the birds survived and thrived excellently. Ever since, I have kept them during the winter in unheated stables, from which they could walk out at any time into the fresh air. So

[1] This chapter was written by Carl Hagenbeck especially for the present translation.

far from having been injured by exposure to the cold, they appear rather to have improved with the treatment. A thicker growth of feathers than normal appeared in response to the new environment.

It is some years ago now since I paid my third visit to the ostrich-farm at Nizza ; and it was after inspecting the contrivances kept there for rearing the chicks that I took the decision to establish an ostrich-farm at Stellingen. It so happened that an assistant, who was engaged at Nizza, asked me in the course of my visit if I could do anything to help him towards attaining a position of greater independence. Great was his surprise when I replied that I had determined to establish for myself an ostrich-farm at Stellingen, and should be happy to engage him as manager. He was at first so doubtful as to the possibility of the success of such an experiment, that he hesitated to accept the proffered post. The climate of Stellingen was bad ; ostriches could only flourish in climates that were dry and sunny ; if bad weather were suddenly to supervene, he knew from experience that the ostriches would quickly be killed. I was well aware, however, that Mr. Millen, for that was his name, had been very successful in hatching out chickens in incubators, and I soon dispelled his apprehensions and engaged him as manager of my prospective ostrich-farm.

A suitable stretch of land (covering an area of more than six acres) lay at my disposal for the purpose ; and in the summer of 1908 we commenced the work of laying it out in accordance with the plans which I proceeded to devise with the help of my son and Mr. Millen. On the 21st June, 1909, the scheme had so far advanced that we were able to take round the German Empress : showing her the first ostrich-farm ever established in the north, as also a young chick just emerged from the egg. Between 20th June and 6th September, 1909, on which date these lines are being written, we have been successful in hatching out no fewer than thirteen African and one American ostriches. These birds are so strong and vigorous that I think there is every hope that we shall be able to bring them up to maturity. From the fourth to the fifth week they actually gained 1 lb. in weight every day.   Although we only have three pairs of breeding birds, we have twenty-two eggs at present in the incubator, most of which apparently have been fertilised ; so we have every reason to be satisfied with the results which we have obtained.   Among the many ostriches

Mr. Millen and the German Emperor with a four-week-old chicken.

which I have recently imported I think there are certain to be ten or twelve good breeding pairs for the coming year, and the prospects for the future appear in consequence very bright.   Let me take the reader on a tour of inspection round the various divisions of the ostrich-farm.

## THE MAIN ENCLOSURE.

We first come to the main building, forty-five yards long by nine yards wide.   On every side of it windows have been

17

inserted, so that, from whichever direction the wind is blowing, ventilation may be secured without the evil of a draught. It has also three exits which can be closed by wooden doors. In connection with this building there is an extensive meadow, serving as an exercise ground and of sufficient size to hold 120 ostriches without undue crowding. In the centre of this meadow we have erected a sheltering roof for the purpose of protecting the food, which is placed under it, from the influence of the weather. There is also supplied a small pond for bathing purposes, which is greatly appreciated by the birds. Various separate enclosures are fenced off at one end of the main enclosure, while, at another end of it, the visitor may see the stalls which are used for breeding purposes. These consist of five small houses with a porch and separate yard attached to each. Each house is further divided into two compartments, so that there are in all ten compartments with a corresponding number of yards, providing comfortable abodes for ten pairs of breeding animals.

Our breeding animals are of course the finest birds that we possess, and are selected with very particular care. Some of those which we have selected, although only two years old, have already attained a height at the top of the back of nearly five feet, and may truly be described as giant birds : but of course I have a few weaklings on my farm, just as other people have. There is, for instance, a hen, coming from an ostrich-farm in South Africa, which has failed to develop properly and shows all the signs of physical degeneration. The ostriches in the farm belong to five geographical varieties—Somali, East African, West African, Cape ostriches, and ostriches from the Abubaama, a tributary of the Blue Nile, these latter including two specially fine cocks.

## THE HOSPITAL.

After passing the separate houses just described, the path leads to another building furnished with projecting eaves, to serve as shelter for sickly or convalescent birds. Here also are placed the animals which have just arrived from foreign parts, so that they may have time to get over the effects of their sea voyage and become used to their new environment, before going loose among the rest.   This is a very necessary precaution ; for if they were placed at once among the other ostriches before becoming accustomed either to the climate or to the food, they would die in a very short time.

### The Chicken-house.

At the conclusion of his round, the visitor arrives at the chicken-house, where the young ostriches are born and pass the first few weeks of their lives.   Part of this chicken-house is separated off from the rest by a glass door, and is devoted to the housing of the incubator.   Here the eggs are kept day and night at an even temperature, and, if the visitor is lucky, he may, perchance, see eggs which are half pecked open by the chickens inside trying to get out.   On the other side of the building there is a long compartment in which the chicks are placed soon after they have been hatched.   It is separated from the visitor by a glass wall, and is partly overgrown with the lucern which acts as food for the chicks. The floor of the chicken-room is covered with sand, and there is an arrangement of hot-water pipes for warming not only the air of the room but also the sand itself.   After they are hatched, the chickens are left for a short time in the incubator and they are then transferred to this chamber. It is very important that the young animals should not be allowed out in the wet, and the chicken-house serves the purpose of a shelter for them in rainy weather.   It is, how-ever, provided with glass doors leading into a clover field, so that they may have opportunities of running about out-side when the weather is sunny.

Many causes concurred in moving me to establish the ostrich-farm at Stellingen.   In the first place there has always been a continuous demand for ostriches from per-sons wishing to establish ostrich-farms abroad.   Previously

I used to find considerable difficulty in meeting this demand. Importation is not only difficult but extremely expensive on account of the large mortality among the birds during transit. The demand has been especially keen during the last four years, in the course of which time I have sold more birds than during the whole previous existence of my firm. I felt therefore under great pressure to set up an establishment at which I could breed the animals myself. Furthermore, I found that many of the ostriches bred in foreign ostrich-farms were very poorly developed and in a degenerate condition ; and I was convinced that this arose from inadequate care in the selection of breeding animals. The point which is especially apt to be neglected is the necessity for the infusion of fresh blood from time to time, thus securing, not only a stronger offspring but a better quality of feathers. Keeping this requirement in mind, I have stocked my farm with over 100 individuals belonging to the five finest varieties of African ostriches in existence. From among these I select only the best for breeding purposes. Besides breeding the pure races, I hope to cross the different varieties with each other so as to secure as wide a range of variation as possible in the progeny. My example has inspired many people, both in Germany and Austria, to make inquiries respecting the management of ostrich-farms. But it will take at least three years before one can tell with certainty the practical outcome of the experiments now being conducted ; and, until that time has expired, I should not encourage any one to enter upon ostrich-farming in our climate from a purely business point of view. If my own enterprise has already turned out to be profitable for me, it does not follow that it would be found profitable also by others ; and I am not yet in a position to say what amount of risk attaches to such undertakings. My chances, however, are certainly better than those of anybody else. In the first place, I am able to take as much as £1,200 a year in entrance fees for the inspection of the ostrich-farm. In the second

The interior of the chicken-house

place, I sell the feathers direct to the purchasers, without the disadvantage of having to pay a commission to English middlemen. In the third place, the sale of the birds which have been bred brings in an annual sum which is not to be despised. These advantages would for the most part not be available in any ordinary farm.

Ostriches begin to breed in their fourth year and the nesting and hatching of the young present many peculiarities. "Nest" indeed is a somewhat euphemistic term to apply to

Just hatched.

the little hollows in the ground where the eggs are laid. This hollow is scraped out by the cock bird with his feet, but not infrequently the hen disregards the preparations of her consort and deposits the eggs without method anywhere on the ground. The cock will then collect the scattered eggs, and roll them all together into the hollow which he has dug out. When three or four have in this way been brought together in the hollow, the hen will of her own accord lay the rest of the clutch in the same place. In the wild state, after the eggs have been laid, they are sat upon by the hen during the day and by the cock at night. They are very large relative to the size of the bird, and contain as much food material as two and a half to three dozen fowls' eggs. The ordinary size of a clutch is from twelve to fifteen eggs. Since, however, we take the eggs as soon as they are laid and put them in the incubator, the hen, relieved by these artificial means of the duty of sitting upon them, will lay as many as thirty good eggs a year.

Incubator with the first chick born at Stellingen, 20th June, 1909.

After the eggs have been placed in the incubator, a period of about six weeks elapses before they are hatched. For the first twenty-four hours after they have been hatched the chicks are allowed to remain in the incubator in order that they may become thoroughly dry. They are then brought into the chamber specially provided for infant ostriches. For the first two days their only food consists of the egg-shells from which they have been hatched, broken up into small pieces. They are then placed upon a diet of lucern, which, as I have already said, is kept in abundant quantities in the chicken-house.   For nearly two months they continue to feed on this green food.   They are allowed to run out of the house on fine days only, and, when the weather is cold or damp, are kept carefully in their house.   In the seventh week after their birth the process of acclimatisation is commenced.   The young birds are taken into a house which has not been artificially heated, and they are allowed to run out even on days when it is cold or damp.   The last four weeks before the moment of writing these lines have been both very cold and wet, and have provided a very severe test of the validity of the method of inuring the young chicks to the climate.   They have, however, passed through it admirably, showing by their gaiety and sprightliness that they are in the best of health.   In the seventh week also they begin to be weaned from their infantine food.   They are given for the first time the same kind of food that is provided for the adults.   This consists of hay chopped up with maize, bran, and barley, mixed together.   Every bird receives in addition 1 lb. of bone daily, broken up in small pieces.   Experience shows that they thrive excellently when treated in this manner.

After six months one is able to gather the first harvest of feathers, and thereafter every nine months a new crop can be taken.   The feathers are cut and not pulled out, so that the process itself is painless to the birds.   The mode of procedure is as follows : The ostrich whose feathers are to be taken is brought out of the farm and has his head enveloped in some kind of a hood, usually a stocking, so that he is unable to watch the operations.   He then generally surrenders himself to his fate.   He is next placed in a wooden vice, which holds him perfectly still, and enables the cutting to be performed without danger to the operator.   The tail and wing feathers are of course the most valuable from the commercial point of view.   They are cut down so that only about two inches of the ends of the quills are left.   The ends ripen in about three months, and are then either plucked out by the birds themselves or removed for them by their keepers. The feathers are sorted immediately they have been cut, those coming from the cocks being kept separate from those coming from the hens. They are all sent off to London, where they are sold by auction and despatched to every part of the world.

It is much to be hoped that, before long, ostrich feathers will come to be considered the most ornamental and useful feathers for ladies' hats. If such a fashion could be introduced, the massacre of many millions of very beautiful and valuable birds would be put an end to. It is high time that this should be done, for the slaughter is rapidly leading to the extinction of some of the most handsome species in the world. This abominable trade is still carried on vigorously in Germany, but I am glad to say that in England the fashions are not quite so barbarous, and ostrich feathers are used to a far greater extent than they are in Germany. The most recent statistics show that South African farmers make from their ostriches a profit of from £2 10s. to £3 each per annum, and in the year 1907 there were exported from Cape Colony alone no less than 598,267 lbs. of ostrich feathers valued at £1,819,668.

There seems no reason why the German colonists in East and South-West Africa should not do as well in this trade as the people of Cape Colony, but it certainly is the case that they do not. There is no sort of reason, moreover, why any of the countries of South America should not do equally well. I have always found that ostriches may be safely kept in large fields in company with quadrupeds, and on the immense prairies of South America, carrying hundreds of thousands of cattle, it would be little extra trouble to the persons in charge of them to maintain large numbers of ostriches at the same time. I am convinced that by this expedient the owners of large herds of cattle could make a considerable increase in their annual profits.

In October, 1903, I received an order from a Rajah in Nepal to send him two pairs of African ostriches. They

arrived safely at their destination, and were then turned loose by the Rajah in his garden. So quickly did they become accustomed to their new surroundings that they at once be-gan to breed, and there was soon a large family of young chickens. In fact they multiplied so fast that the Rajah,

Riding an ostrich.

some time afterwards, wanted to sell some of them to one of my agents who was travelling in Nepal last year. I did not take them, however. What with the long journey and high freight the transaction could not have been profitable, even if he had presented them to me free of charge. I only now narrate the story in order to show how, in a favourable climate, the birds will thrive and multiply abundantly, with scarcely any care or observation.

The natives of the Sudan and of Somaliland are thoroughly acquainted with the art of hatching out the eggs of wild ostriches. This they do by a sort of natural system of incubation, in place of the artificial system prevailing among Europeans. They make a shallow hollow in the ground, and after having collected the eggs, they place them in this hollow, taking care that they do not come into contact with one another. The intervening spaces are then filled up with loose sand or with doura, so that the eggs are entirely covered up. As shelter from the fierce rays of the sun, a few branches are thrown together over the hollow. From time to time the eggs are turned round, so that they are warmed equally on every side. By this method several of my travellers, and especially Menges, have hatched out eggs in the Sudan. The young have usually thriven well, and in most cases have been successfully transported to Europe.

Some years ago a number of ostrich eggs were brought to a friend of mine, who was living in Somaliland. He happened to be busy at the time, and, putting them into his desk, went away and forgot all about them. About a fortnight later he had occasion to go again to his desk, but, on opening it, he started back in terror, crying out for some one to bring him a stick, for that there was a snake in his desk and he wanted to kill it. A stick was brought, and the desk again very cautiously opened; upon which there emerged instead of the terrible reptile, which he had anticipated, the head and neck of an ostrich chick just escaped from its egg-shell. Nothing more need be said to show how little care or trouble is needed to hatch out these animals in suitable climates. In such countries the natives give them for food large quantities of meat and also some bone. They feed on green vegetable food as well; and in Somaliland in particular upon a creeping plant called armo.

Ostriches are hunted in several different ways. In Somaliland the common method is to use a female bird as a
decoy. A cord several hundred yards long is tied to the
decoy bird, and she is then taken out to the districts which
the wild ostriches are known to frequent. On reaching the
scene of action, the huntsman conceals himself behind a bush,
and, holding the end of the cord in his hand, lets the female
ostrich go free. The wild cock birds are soon attracted

Driving an ostrich.

towards her, and when they are together the huntsman
gradually hauls in the cord so that the wild birds, unwitting
of their danger, are slowly brought nearer to their mortal foe.
Thirty or forty yards is near enough for the huntsman's purpose. At that distance they are well within arrow range, and
he proceeds to shoot them with a poisoned dart. The arrow
is perfectly noiseless in its flight through the air, and the
bird which has been struck makes little disturbance ; but after
a short time the poison takes effect upon him and he quietly

succumbs. In this way nothing happens to alarm the other birds in the neighbourhood, and half a dozen are often slain one after the other. If a gun had been used, the whole flock would of course have been scared away at the first discharge.

The Bushmen in South Africa hunt ostriches somewhat differently. They cover their heads and bodies with the skins of dead ostriches, so that when walking along they much resemble real ostriches. They can thus approach to within close distance of a flock and shoot the birds with their poisoned arrows. The Bedouins hunt ostriches by riding them down with swift horses—a sport of which they are very fond. One of my huntsmen on a journey to the interior once rode down and killed with a sword no fewer than three male ostriches in succession, without changing his horse.

To persons considering the possibility of establishing ostrich-farms, my advice would be to begin with only a few breeding pairs, so that, if their inexperience should lead to failure, the loss will not be on too large a scale. This, I may mention, is the course recommended by the Government of Cape Colony to the farmers in that country. Although by this method success can only come slowly, it is likely to be much more sure, for an ambitious beginning usually results in a premature end. It will perhaps be objected to my proposal for the establishment of so many ostrich-farms, that the supply of feathers would soon outrun the demand, and that therefore their value would sink so as to render the business unprofitable. To this my reply is that I have little doubt that before long laws will be passed in civilised countries for prohibiting the importation of feathers from ornamental birds for ladies' hats. An immediate result of such legislation would be that the demand for and consequently the value of ostrich feathers would rapidly increase ; so that there is little danger that this commodity will ever become a drug on the market.

# CHAPTER XII.

## ANTHROPOID APES.

THE anthropoid apes have always been particular favourites of mine ; and I have at all times endeavoured to secure as large a number of these interesting animals as possible. This foible of mine has in fact cost me considerable sums : for the apes, in their natural state, live in moist tropical regions and suffer very much from the severity of our northern latitudes. But in spite of this, I have been very successful with these creatures, and am especially proud of a fine pair of orang-outangs called Jacob and Rosa, and also of a clever chimpanzee called Moritz, who have by this time become quite well-known personages in the town of Hamburg. The two orangs I purchased from a farmer, who got them in Borneo when they were quite young, and brought them up on the bottle. For seven years they were kept in captivity in Borneo. Captivity, however, is perhaps hardly the word, for they had complete liberty, and were treated as though they were members of the family. They used always to have their mid-day meal at table with their master, eating precisely the same food as he did himself. They were in short treated just like children, and very polite and well-behaved children too. On their voyage to Europe they were treated more like passengers than apes. At all times they were free to wander about on board, and they speedily became the pets of all the ship's crew. Since they had so long been accustomed to freedom I realised the danger of placing them, when they came to my animal park, in undue restraint or in a cramped and badly ventilated cage. I therefore

procured a special waggon-cage, the walls of which were on
every side formed only by bars. On the north and east
sides canvas was stretched to provide protection from the

Such is life.

weather. In the waggon-cage a large closed-in wooden box
was placed, which the animals could go into at night. In
this way I was able to keep them all through the summer of

Two orangs taking a constitutional.

1907. I feared, however, that the creatures would suffer from the loss of the society to which they had been accustomed; so I told off one of my keepers to the sole duty of minding them and remaining constantly with them. I hoped thus to ward off the ill effects of the tediousness of their life, and my hope was amply justified. The animals not only continued to thrive on the physical side, but showed great development on the mental side as well. When the cold season arrived, I thought it inadvisable to keep them any longer in the open waggon-cage and I therefore had a compartment erected in the giraffe house for them to pass the winter in.

Some time after the acquisition of these two orangs, Moritz made his appearance. He is a male chimpanzee, about seven years old, and he quickly made friends with the orangs. The three anthropoids passed the winter together most satisfactorily in the giraffe house. We took care to ventilate the building thoroughly by means of windows placed high up near the roof, so that the temperature there was never tropical. On the return of summer, I devised a cage for them from which they could emerge at any time into the open air. I still kept them in the giraffe house, but I set aside a portion of the open enclosure of the giraffes for their use  The cages in which they were confined communicated with the enclosure by means of doors, which opened by being merely pushed, and then closed again by their own weight. The apes soon learnt to push open the doors when they wanted to get out. In both the inner cage and the outer enclosure gymnastic appliances were set up, so that the creatures should have plenty of opportunity for amusing themselves. They are very fond of fun, and in their sports I have seen much that is interesting and amusing. I ought to say at once that the naturally high capacities of anthropoids are greatly enhanced by constant association with human beings, and never fully develop except in such association. The chimpanzee is far the most vivacious and mischievous of the three. He is always the ringleader in the various pranks and tricks which they play, the orangs merely following him out of friendship.    One of his favourite tricks is to snatch hats from ladies and gentlemen who have come to look at him, and then retire with his booty to a gym-

Diogenes.

nastic pole fixed in his cage.    In order to carry out this knavish trick he has to exercise a remarkable degree of cunning.    He takes advantage of a habit, which the orangs have acquired, of holding out their hands to greet visitors when they come up.    Sitting quietly near the front of the cage he appears to be taking no notice of anything, but when a visitor reaches forward to shake hands with the orang, he dashes with lightning speed at his hat, and seizing it with a dexterous grasp whisks it off to the gymnastic bar. The sequel to these performances was not so pleasant, for me at least, as the performances themselves. I got tired after a time of having to pay for new hats every day, and I was reduced to the necessity of putting up a barrier between the apes and the public.

Somali child with orang-outang.

Even that, however, I found insufficient. The public were in the habit of giving the creatures food, which was very unwholesome, and on two occasions brought them in danger of their lives. To prevent this I finally had a glass wall set up to shut them off completely from visitors.

Moritz very easily becomes bored when the keeper goes away; and in order to relieve his feelings is much addicted to practical jokes. He is very fond of singling out the orang Jacob as a butt for his humour. When the latter is off his

guard, he will jump suddenly upon his head in an endeavour
to knock him over. A hand-to-hand scuffle immediately
ensues, in which Moritz always comes off best, on account
of his superior agility. He quickly escapes from the clutches
of the orang, and a few leaps take him to the other end of
the cage. He is followed clumsily and deliberately by the
larger animal, but is never caught. As the orang does not
leap, he is never able to catch his tormentor, who keeps just
out of reach.

In his many attempts to escape from captivity, Moritz is
most ingenious and amusing. When we shut off a corner of
the giraffe house for the use of the apes, we did not think it
necessary to carry the partition right up to the roof. The
house, having been built to accommodate giraffes, was of
course very high, and it never occurred to us as possible that
the apes might succeed in scaling the wooden partition which
we erected. Nevertheless Moritz did succeed in doing so.
When the keeper came along one day, he found the chimpanzee among the giraffes, and could not imagine how he
had got there. He afterwards found that he had employed
the following device: Up against the wooden partition stood
a wooden box which served as a sleeping place for the apes.
There was also kept in the cage a large tin globe. Moritz
had acquired a considerable influence over the lady orang,
Rosa, and he persuaded her to assist him in his efforts to
escape. By their united strength, they were able to push the
tin globe over to the sleeping box and set it on the top.
When this had been done Rosa stood upon the globe, up
against the wall, while Moritz climbed up on her shoulders.
From there he was just able by a vigorous bound to reach
the top of the partition with his hands. It was then scarcely
the work of a moment to draw himself up, and drop gently
among the giraffes. These animals paid little attention to the
chimpanzee, but if they came near him he would throw something at them as a hint to mind their own business. When we
had discovered the method of the ape's escape, we thought we

would effectually prevent it occurring again, by carrying the partition some way higher. Moritz, however, was not to be outwitted; and his ingenuity was sufficient to overcome this further obstacle. Among the gymnastic arrangements set up for his use, was a long rope hanging from the ceiling. By climbing some way up it, and giving it a swing backwards

Learning to kiss.

and forwards, he was able to bring himself within measurable distance of the top of the partition; and by an adroit leap, at exactly the right moment, to secure a footing on the top. Finally, we were obliged to carry the partition the whole way up to the roof, in order to keep the animal securely con‐ fined. He still, however, had his thoughts set on escaping. He used to watch the keeper with interest when the latter inserted his key in the lock, in order to open the cage. The keeper would often give him the keys to play about with, and on one occasion he took advantage of this to try them one after another in the lock of the door, to find out which one it was that fitted it. After a time the right key was hit upon, and the ape succeeded after several efforts in turning the latch and opening the door. When I happened to come along and was told what had occurred, I went to see the ape in his cage, and asked him half jokingly, "how did you manage to do this?" He had all the appearance of understanding the tenor of my question, for he smiled slyly and held up the key as if to say that that was what he did it with.

The intelligence of my anthropoids is by no means confined to Moritz, for Jacob on one occasion was equally successful in finding an exit from the cage. It so happened that one day a piece of an iron rod had accidentally been broken off by the creatures from one of the gymnastic appliances inserted in their cage. Jacob took this piece of iron, and proceeded to utilise it for bursting the lock. By inserting it into the ring of the padlock, with their united strength they were able to exercise so much leverage that the padlock gave way. The cage door was opened and all three gained their liberty. What further evidence could be required of the high intelligence which these animals possess? Rosa, too, was not behindhand in devising means of escape. The outer cage of the apes was constructed of wire, and her method was to loosen the wire from its fastening, and so break away an opening large enough for her to pass through. She had, often before, been taken out of the cage by the keeper, and led round to the main entrance into the animal park to be given some bananas, which used to be sold there; and now when she had escaped she made rapidly for the main entrance of her own accord without hesitating for a moment as to the correct route, hoping no doubt to secure there some of her coveted bananas.

To a lover of animals nothing can be more interesting

than watching these great apes while at their food. For breakfast they are given not only succulent fruits such as bananas, but also bread and milk. For their mid-day meal they have precisely the same food as is served to me in my own house. They are not very dainty in their appetites, but like solid homely food, and devour it with great relish. At

Having dinner.

times they are given good red wine mixed with water, a beverage of which Jacob is decidedly fond, though Rosa with her more ladylike instincts cares little for it. Their manners at table are now perfectly refined and proper. Moritz acts as the waiter. He has to bring in the food, which he does with great pomp and ceremony, and he has to clear away the things again after the meal is over. During the repast the apes sit patiently on chairs drawn up to the table, and await

the various courses which are served to them.  They eat
after the manner of human beings with spoons and forks, and
they are very clever at ladling up their soup with the spoon.
It is true that if they thought no one was looking, they would
quickly revert to more expeditious methods, dispensing with
the spoon and using their lips instead ; but a word from the

Two orangs drinking soup.

keeper immediately recalls them to the manners of civilisation,
and the spoon is hastily seized once more.

All the apes are of course thoroughly amenable to the
control of the keeper.  He knows how to make himself understood by them, and they on their part watch him attentively
and carry out intelligently whatever instructions he delivers to
them.  Jacob and Rosa are especially amenable in this respect.  They are very sensitive to verbal censure, and of

course still more sensitive to corporal punishment.  Moritz, on the other hand, is a more thick-skinned and robust animal ; not so easily controlled by either mode of reproof.  The keeper finds it necessary, therefore, when he has to be made to do something, to keep at hand a stick on which the ape's attention may constantly fall.
When, for instance, he has
to be photographed, he is
seized with an irresistible
inclination to walk up to the
camera and gaze into it from
a distance which makes it
impossible to take his like-
ness.   He requires a good
deal of cajoling before he
can be persuaded to take
up a proper pose.   The
chimpanzee in these re-
spects is just the opposite
of the phlegmatic orang.
Unlike the orang, he is a
sanguine sort of individual,
and very mercurial in temperament, changing in a
moment from the brightest
gaiety to the deepest de-
spondency, and *vice versâ.*

Bill, please, walter !

He can never keep his atten-
tion fixed on one thing for more than a moment or two, but is constantly flying off at a tangent to some new idea which has taken his fancy.   His latest craze has been learning how to ride a bicycle.   It took him only a few weeks to perform this feat, and he now rides astonishingly well.   He appears to find it great fun, moreover, and pedals about with such vigour in my animal park that the trainer is hard put to it to keep up with him.

For looking after these anthropoids I have secured a

young Englishman, very efficient at his work ; and it is his business to carry forward the education of the animals to the highest possible extent.    The conviction has gradually

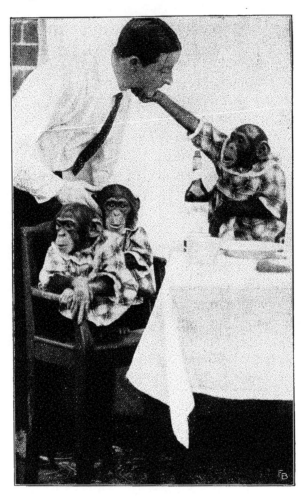

An egg, please, uncle dear !

strengthened within me that anthropoid apes may, by a systematic education from their earliest youth, be accustomed to live just like human beings.    And I intend to proceed with my experiments aiming at the realisation of this idea.    Inti-mate association with human beings is the proper method of going to work. It would of course be fatal with such highly organised creatures to endeavour to educate them by general principles alone. One ape differs very much from another, and the peculiarities of each have to be carefully watched and made the most of. It is no less necessary for a trainer to bear in mind the idiosyncrasies of the animals which he has to deal with, than it is for a human teacher to take note of the idiosyn-

Gorillas suffering from home-sickness.

crasies of his pupils. Above all things, tact and patience are necessary in a high degree. I am hoping before long to be able to exhibit such educational results in my apes as have never been achieved or even thought possible before.

In order to keep the great apes in sound health, it is necessary to provide them with plenty of society, either of their own species or of some other. In the case of all animals in captivity, it is of the first importance to take measures for combating the tedium from which they would otherwise suffer.

But it is more than ever necessary in the case of such highly
organised animals as anthropoid apes. When they are constantly playing about together, with plenty of stimulus to keep
them always on the move, their digestion is kept in good
order, their appetite maintained, and a high tone preserved
throughout the system. They are especially subject to psychical influences ; and, the more they are kept in contact with
human beings, the more likely are they to thrive and forget
their captivity.

I feel pretty confident that it is mental depression, and
not any physical ailment, which makes it so difficult to keep
gorillas for any length of time in captivity. None of those
which have come to me have ever survived for long their
arrival in Europe. They show every day a gradually dim-
inishing interest in their surroundings, until at last they refuse
food altogether and are found dead one morning in their cage
It is true that there have been instances now and again of
gorillas being kept for a considerable period in captivity, but
such cases are only exceptions. Perhaps in the course of
time I shall succeed in discovering the proper method of
treating these great apes. At present I have learnt little
of them except the conviction that their trouble is psychical
and not physical. It has hitherto been the almost universal
habit to credit gorillas, and for the matter of that chimpanzees
and orangs too, with much less intensity of feeling than they
actually possess.

Their memories at least are undeniably excellent. After
the two orangs had been in my possession for a period of
twelve months, their former owner came to the park to see
them. They instantly recognised him and showed their
pleasure in the most unmistakable manner. One may observe in these creatures the origin of the capacity for laughter.
When they are amused the corners of the mouth move outwards, showing the teeth between their lips. In Moritz
particularly, the play of the expressions on the countenance
is very noticeable. The keeper can tell at a glance,

The three friends.

from the expression in his eye, what sort of a mood he is in. His memory, like that of the orang, is excellent. Some time ago, after I had been travelling for some time and had just returned, I went to see him in his cage. The moment I set foot in the ape-house he welcomed me with loud shouts, and would not be pacified until I had gone into his cage, and taken him in my arms and fondled him.

In June, 1908, Lieutenant Heinicke of the German army brought over with him from Kamerun a young gorilla which was taken round to be introduced to my three anthropoids. Their meeting was very interesting and unique. The gorilla displayed only a moderate interest in his three cousins, taking, in plain words, very little notice of them. They, on the other hand, were immensely interested and excited. The chimpanzee gave vent to his feelings in loud yells ; and thrusting his arms through the bars tried to draw the gorilla towards him. When he failed in this attempt, he became indignant, and proceeded to pelt the stranger with sand and stones. The orangs likewise endeavoured to reach the gorilla through the bars ; and, when they failed, expressed their emotions, each according to his kind. Jacob followed the example of the chimpanzee and began throwing stones ; while Rosa's excitement brought on a fit of vomiting, so that the whole scene was indescribably droll. The scene was in other ways almost unique. For here there were gathered together in one spot representatives of the three species of animals most nearly akin to man.

Lieutenant Heinicke, who had brought the young gorilla to Europe in the society of two negro boys, hoped to be able to keep this rare animal alive for a long time. Over in Kamerun he had kept it for more than a year, during which time it had enjoyed unbroken health and become a general pet of the station. He hoped to be able to overcome the difficulty of lack of society by providing the two negroes as constant associates for the animal. When the ape first arrived at my animal park he was much weakened with his long sea voyage and took little interest in anything that was going on round about, but he soon picked up, and after a time would sit and walk about on the lawn in company with his two play-fellows, apparently in the best of health and spirits. He had a strong predilection for the petals of roses, and would consume large quantities of them. When he had to be taken from one place to another one of the negroes used to carry him on his back, presenting a very droll appearance.

Here, then, I must conclude my account of the many animal friendships that I have formed in the course of my life. I am continuing to develop my park on the lines already followed ; and trust that, both in the exhibits of wild beasts and in those of wild men, I shall ever succeed more com-pletely in rendering it, not a place of captivity, but a happy and contented home. With the help of an able staff of assistants, whose experience now extends over several de-cades, I hope to make my institution unique in all the world as a centre for the friendly intercourse of great gatherings of BEASTS AND MEN.

# INDEX.

INDEX 295

Eggenschwyler, Urs, 106.
Eland antelopes. *See under* Antelopes.
Elephants, hunting of, in the Sudan, 51-53; in Abyssinia, 70; intelligence and individual peculiarities of, 147-53; a dangerous individual, 154, 155; vitality of a sick, 156, 157; adaptability of, to training, 159; successful training of African species, 160-62; cure of a sick, 222.
Eskimo, visit of, to Germany, 20, 25; description of, 21, 22.
Ewart, James Cossar, his experiments in the crossing of zebras and horses, 219.
Extermination (of wild species), approaching problem of, 212; a project to avoid, 215.

Falz-Fein, M. (naturalist), his specimens of the Mongolian wild horse, 74; success of, in acclimatisation, 212; experiments of, in crossbreeding, 219.
Feathers, ostrich, cutting of, 265, 266.
Florida, ideal site for an animal reserve, 215.
Forepaugh, a menagerie owner and rival of Barnum, 26.
Fraser, Sir Thomas R., interest of, in serpent's venom, 196.
Funk, M., director of Cologne Zoological Gardens, 111, 112.

Garner, Professor, his monkey-language, 61.
Gipsies, cruelty of, to bears, 226-28.
Giraffes, difficulty in stabling, 173; subject to a peculiar disease, 174, 175; first appearance of, in Europe, 175; acclimatisation of, 204; reference to, 212, 216.
Glanders, appearance of, among Hagenbeck's animals, 35.
Gorillas, subject to mental depression, 204, 288.
Grieger, Wilhelm, account of his expedition in search of Mongolian wild horse, 74-89.

Hagenbeck, Carl, birth and early education of, 2-5; he decides to be an animal dealer, 7; contract of, with Cassanova, and transport of his collection, 8, 11-14; marriage of, and removal to Neuer Pferdemarkt, 15; origin of his ethnographic exhibitions, 16; the Lapps, 16-20; the Eskimo and others, 20-25; the Cingalese exhibition, 29; his humane method of animal training, 30-32, 37, 121; expansion of his business, 38, 41, 42; purchase and development of land at Stellingen, 39-45; relations of, with pet carnivores, 98-106; incident of the pickled lion, 122, 123; on study of the individual animal, 125; and careful selection of performers, 126; details of his method of training, 126-34; first experiences of, in training, 139, 140; experiments of, in association of naturally hostile animals, 143, 144; adventure of, with cow-elephant, 148-51; and with bull-elephant, 151-53; "Bosco," 158, 159; adventure of, with a rhinoceros, 165-67; and with a hippopotamus, 171, 172; experiences of,

Printed in Great Britain
by Amazon

68723186R00181